PARADISE BY THE RIVER

PARADISE BY THE RIVER

The Story of Petawawa
An Historical Drama in Three Acts

Vittorio Rossi

Talonbooks
1998

Copyright © 1998 Vittorio Rossi
Published with the assistance of the Canada Council.

Talonbooks
#104—3100 Production Way
Burnaby, British Columbia, Canada V5A 4R4

Typeset in New Baskerville and printed and bound in Canada by
Hignell Printing.

First Printing: September 1998

Talonbooks are distributed in Canada by General Distribution
Services, 325 Humber College Blvd., Toronto, Ontario, Canada
M9W 7C3; Tel.:(416) 213-1919; Fax:(416) 213-1917.

Talonbooks are distributed in the U.S.A. by General Distribution
Services Inc., 85 Rock River Drive, Suite 202, Buffalo, New York,
U.S.A. 14207-2170; Tel.:1-800-805-1083; Fax:1-800-481-6207.

Canadian Cataloguing in Publication Data

Rossi, Vittorio, 1961-
    Paradise by the river

    A play.
    ISBN 0-88922-393-9

    I. Title.
PS8585.O8425P37 1998   C812'.54   C98-910726-4
PR9199.3.R69P37 1998

For my father Silvio,
the master storyteller.

Paradise By The River opened on April 30, 1998 at the Centaur Theatre in Montréal. It was presented by Ciro Cucciniello & Frank Calandriello, Di Ioia & Associates, Avicor Construction Inc. and Belmonte Léger et Associés, in cooperation with the H.B. Arts Foundation and Rossi Production, with the following cast:

ROMANO ....Mark Camacho

MARIA...Penny Mancuso

CENZO ....Tony Nappo

HÉLÈNE ....Nathalie Breuer

LORENZO/CALO ....Louis Tucci

BRUNO/M. BEAUCHAMP.................Harry Standjofski

LT-COL. LUCERNE/
RCMP OFFICER 1/STORE OWNER ....Ted Whittall

SGT. DUNNISON/RCMP OFFICER 2/
MAN 1/POLICEMAN ....Henry Gauthier

VITO/LEFEBVRE/MAN 2 ....Carlo Berardinucci

LUCA...John Aprea

Director: Joel Miller
Producers: Bruce Johnson and Vittorio Rossi
Set and Costume Designer: Guido Tondino
Lighting Designer: Freddie Grimwood
Production Manager/Technical Director: Steve Schön
General Manager: Susan Fuda
Stage Manager: Johanne Pomrenski
Apprentice Stage Manager: Lisa Cochran

The author would like to thank the Canada Council Arts Award service for providing a grant for the writing of this play.

CHARACTERS

Romano Dicenzo, 34 years old, a stone mason.
Maria Dicenzo, 28 years old, his wife, a seamstress.
Cenzo Dicenzo, 32 years old, Romano's brother, a carpenter.
Hélène Beauchamp, mid thirties, the Dicenzo's neighbour.
Bruno Benevento, early forties, Maria's cousin.
M. Beauchamp, Hélène's father.
Lorenzo, a grocery store owner, speaks Italian in the Calabrese dialect.
Lieutenant-Colonel Robert Lucerne, Royal Canadian Army, commandant of Camp Petawawa.
Staff Sergeant Bill Dunnison, Royal Canadian Army, camp censor.
Luca Delferro, a 50-year-old Sicilian, a prisoner.
Calo Calabrese, a 35-year-old Calabrese, a musician, a prisoner.
Vito Di Napoli, 18 years old, a prisoner.
M. Lefebvre, a lawyer.
3 RCMP officers, 1 Montréal Police officer, a store owner, a guard, a judge, 2 thugs.

PLACE

Various places in Montréal. Camp Petawawa, Ontario. Gagetown, New Brunswick.

TIME

The play takes place from 1940 to 1945.

Note: Where Italian and French dialogue appear, an English translation will appear in square brackets [ ].

ACT ONE

Scene 1

May 10, 1940. A backyard in Ville Émard, Montréal. HÉLÈNE BEAUCHAMP is standing on a chair, as MARIA DICENZO is basting the hem of her dress. MARIA is a woman of 28, her strong and deft movements belie her sultry and sensual exterior. HÉLÈNE is in her early thirties, a hard-working woman who has kept her sensual disposition. She wears a lovely dress which accentuates her sexual appeal. BRUNO, a man in his early forties, stands about. Over this action we hear the evening news over the sound system.

RADIO ANNOUNCER: Good evening, this is Duane Murphy with the six o'clock evening news: May 10, 1940. In a stunning development in the war in Europe, Nazi Germany has invaded The Netherlands, Belgium, and Luxembourg. Due to the escalation of the war Prime Minister Neville Chamberlain of England has resigned. Winston Churchill is due to take over. In London today there was talk of Italy's possible involvement in the war. There was no comment from Rome, but Churchill said in no uncertain terms that Italy's involvement would be a mistake and prove to be fatal.

MARIA: (*overlapping*) Did you hear that?

BRUNO: Sshhh.

RADIO ANNOUNCER: (*continuing*) So far, President Roosevelt has yet to comment on the matter. A British member of parliament however was quoted as saying: "It would be a sad day indeed if Britain and Italy were to break their traditional alliance."

HÉLÈNE: (*overlapping*) It won't happen.

BRUNO: Will you be quiet.

RADIO ANNOUNCER: (*continuing*) Prime Minister Mackenzie King was asked what he would do should Italy join forces with Germany. Said the Prime Minister: "Plans are already afoot should that day come." In other news today....

BRUNO: Well the lines are drawn now, you heard it. How are you supposed to live like this?

MARIA: Bruno, you're blocking the light, get out of the way.

HÉLÈNE: Le monde est paranoïaque. Il faut se calmer. So long as the war is in Europe, we'll be fine. It's all happening so far away.
[The world is paranoid. We have to calm down]

MARIA: Hélène, ne bouges pas. S'il vous plait.
[Hélène, don't move. Please.]

BRUNO: Your French is getting better.

HÉLÈNE: Che bella giornata oggi. Io sono molto contenta.
[What a beautiful day today. I am very happy.]

BRUNO: Hey, Hélène, you keep talking like that people might mistake you for an Italian.

HÉLÈNE: You think so?

BRUNO: No.

MARIA: Hélène, I need precision now.... I'm almost done....

HÉLÈNE: ...Sorry. Did you notice those two men down the street? They don't seem to be from the neighbourhood. All day long, up and down the street. Looking here, looking there. What do they want?

BRUNO: They look like a couple of city inspectors. (*pause*) Did you talk to Romano? Maria, I'm just asking for a little decency here. We've been working together for five years. My reputation as a bricklayer travels the whole city. I have to refuse work. Do you understand what I'm saying?

MARIA: My husband runs the company, it's his business, you bring it up with him.

BRUNO: I know the two of you talk—The competition is getting stiff out there. He can't do it alone.

MARIA: He's not.

BRUNO: So there it is, Romano will bring his brother into the company, and Cenzo, who has no idea how things work in this city, is going to help him run it.

HÉLÈNE: Why don't you start your own company?

BRUNO: Hélène, please, you run a grocery store, stay out of this.

HÉLÈNE: You know, Bruno, you're just like the bricks you lay, straight and to the point.

BRUNO: You people have no idea what's going on in this world. You live in your small little minds, you carry on totally oblivious to the call. The call for change. The world is getting smaller, so business has to get bigger. You do that by putting together the proper talent.

HÉLÈNE: You're a bricklayer.

BRUNO: And you're having a dress made by an Italian.

MARIA: Will you both stop it. I've said my piece, anything else, bring it up with Romano.

BRUNO: My talents are underestimated by that man. I swear…sometimes I think the Fascists have had it right all along.

HÉLÈNE: So now you're going to tell me that Fascism is the answer?

BRUNO: The mayor thinks so. And he's French. Look at Germany's recovery. Could we have done that here? And Mussolini? Hasn't he given us our pride back?

HÉLÈNE: Are you a Fascist?

BRUNO: I didn't say that. But I can see the change.

LORENZO: (*entering*) Buona sera a tutti. Maria, Romano ancora non'arrivato?
[Good evening to all. Maria, Romano hasn't arrived yet?]

MARIA: Tra poco. Teresina non c'é fatta vedere oggi.
[Soon. Teresina hasn't shown herself today.]

LORENZO: Di quando arrivama a stu paesi, e diventata comu n'americana. Ancora curcata e! Bruno, va dire na cosa, io l'unglese lo capiscu ciu e meno zero. Pero dave na parola che la sentu sempre. Dimmi, chi vola dire, Fuck? Tutti sti ragazzi intorna'me, trasano co u storu e dicano, Fuck Fuck Fuck. Fucka you, fuckame, che cazzo.
[Since we've arrived in this country, she's become just like an American. She's still taking a nap! Bruno, tell me, I understand English very little. But there is this word that I hear all the time. Tell me, What does Fuck mean? All these kids around me, they enter the store and they say, Fuck Fuck Fuck. Fucka you, fuckame, what the hell.]

BRUNO: Lorenzo, e una parola dispregativo.
[Lorenzo, it's a swear word.]

HÉLÈNE: En anglais c'est pas un mot très gentil.
[In English it's not a very nice word.]

LORENZO: Ah, capiscu. Allora: Buon giorno Fuck non si puo dire?
[Ah, I understand. So: Good morning Fuck you can't say?]

ROMANO: (*offstage*) Maria! Maria!

MARIA: (*overlapping*) They've arrived! We're out back!

ROMANO enters the backyard. He is a charming and strong-willed man of 34 years.

MARIA: Where's Cenzo?

ROMANO: The train pulled in. I waited, I never saw him.

MARIA: His letter said he'd be here today.

ROMANO: He'll be on the next train. Don't worry about it. Mademoiselle Beauchamp, comment allez-vous?
[Miss Beauchamp, how are you?]

HÉLÈNE: Maria, we could finish this later. (*to ROMANO*) Bien, merci. Et vous?
[Fine, thank you. and you?]

MARIA: (*overlapping*) No, no, I'm almost done. (*MARIA resumes working on HÉLÈNE's dress*)

LORENZO: Romano, ecco l'assegno per l'accontu da casa nova. Vi dite cha a casa a vogliu chu la cantina.
[Romano, here is the cheque for the down payment on the new house. I want a house with a wine cellar.]

ROMANO: Non ti preoccupare.
[Don't worry about it.]

LORENZO: Va bene. (*shouts off*) Teresina! Ti aspetto d'avanti! Salutamo. (*exits*)
[Alright. Teresina! I'll wait for you out front! Good evening to all.]

BRUNO: You're accepting a down payment on a house you haven't built yet?

ROMANO: That's the way business is done, Bruno.

BRUNO: You said you were going to talk to me before your brother arrives.

ROMANO: Don't, don't start with that. No means no. I'm not interested. Hélène, your father's looking for you. You just got another delivery of fruit.

HÉLÈNE: C'est pas possible. These late deliveries are killing us.

ROMANO: Why don't you just take the fruit off the trucks, you stock the empty shelves tomorrow. That way you could join us for dinner.

HÉLÈNE: Let me talk to my father first.

MARIA: There. It's done.

HÉLÈNE: (*gets down from the chair, and shows off her dress*) Look at me!

MARIA: Let me see. Turn around. Oh, Hélène, you're so beautiful!

HÉLÈNE: How do you do it? You're an artist, you know that? Une vraie artiste! You have to make me another one. I feel like a new woman! I'm like a child again!

BRUNO: When are you going to make me that new shirt I asked for?

MARIA: (*checks the dress for any defects*) Get me the material and you'll have your shirt.

ROMANO: Why doesn't Rita learn how to make her own clothes?

BRUNO: Me, I'd be happy if she knew how to boil me an egg.

MARIA: I can take it in a quarter inch. You're losing weight. You're not eating.

HÉLÈNE: I'm on my feet all day.

ROMANO: I can't believe you're still single. In Italy, a woman like you would have men all over her. Isn't that right, Bruno? (*honking is heard from offstage*) That's your father.

HÉLÈNE: I better get going.

MARIA: You can't leave with this dress, it's just a temporary hem.

HÉLÈNE: I'll show my father, and maybe I can get off work. (*gives her the bag*) Here.

MARIA: Hélène, you didn't have to.

HÉLÈNE: It's the least I could do. You're such an angel. I don't know what I'd do without you. (*more honking*) Oui, papa! J'arrive!
[Yes, papa! I'm coming!]

ROMANO: I have the rent money. (*hands her some money*) If you don't make it in time for dinner, at least come by for coffee.

HÉLÈNE: (*more honking*) I'll try. Well what is it you say? Buon pranzo?

ROMANO: Si, si, grazie.

HÉLÈNE: Ciao. (*exits into the house*)

BRUNO: You let her go through the house like that? You never know, she sees something she likes— bing!—in her pocket it goes. Look at this. You make her a dress, she gives you some fruit. Apples! Apples don't cost anything here. Don't let her take advantage of you.

MARIA: She's my friend, I trust her. Show her some respect! (*pause*) What are you going to do about Cenzo?

ROMANO: Next train is not due for another hour. Are you eating with us?

BRUNO: Rita is waiting for me. Let me know when Cenzo gets in. If it's not too late, we'll go to Bar Roma for a coffee…we'll talk….

ROMANO: Talk about what?

BRUNO: Romano, why are you pushing me away like this? I've put five years into this. Your brother hops off a train, and he's running a company? Maria, don't you see the problem here?

ROMANO: Don't do this to Maria! You want to talk business, you come to me! You are a real work of art, you know, that Fascist talk at the construction bid last month almost cost me the contract. And you're telling me how to run a business? You talk this nonsense, I lose contracts, and we don't eat. Get this through your head: you're a bricklayer. Accept it. And live with it.

BRUNO: Fine. We'll never agree on this. It's your company, do what you want with it. You think that I can't contribute to your company as an equal partner…don't come running to me for help. There's competition out there, just remember that.

ROMANO: You don't want to work for me anymore?

BRUNO: (*pause*) I'll get going.

MARIA: Here. (*gives BRUNO some of the apples*) Give these to Rita. We have enough here.

BRUNO: I'll see you later. (*exits*)

MARIA: I don't see why the two of you can't come to an agreement.

ROMANO: He doesn't know how to deal with business. You should hear him talking on the job, you'd swear he's a Fascist. He turns around, he's a Communist. He doesn't even know what political game to play. I can't have business people worried about that.

MARIA: There's something you're not telling me. What is it?

ROMANO: I was going to wait until the deal was final. My lawyer, Mr. Lefebvre, has just put together a land deal for me. Five acres in Ville LaSalle. It's prime property. Houses will have to be built, you know how much work that means? Do you know how big we're going to be? Do you see now why I don't want Bruno involved? Once I'm on the top, I'll work him in. (*pause*) What's wrong? (*he goes to embrace her*) Have I ever failed you? Look at me.

MARIA: Look how much we've sacrificed because of your company. We don't even own our own home. I thought it was family first.

ROMANO: It is. Do you want me to just throw it all away now? Now that I have Cenzo, the company will expand by three times. I'll need to hire more men. We'll call over your cousins, your brother. Together we'll build houses all over Montréal. How was work?

MARIA: The clothes they make here, there's no style. It's all so ordinary.

ROMANO: Tell that to the foreman. You're a dressmaker, not just some ordinary seamstress.

MARIA: You want me lose my job?

ROMANO: If you don't speak up, they'll walk all over you. We came to Canada because of the opportunities, now you want us to sit by while everyone else gets rich and we stay poor? (*He kisses her. She embraces him strongly, as they continue kissing. He feels her stomach*) What does it feel like? A boy or a girl? (*she kisses him*) You know what today is? It was five years ago today that we became Canadian citizens. Five years. We are Canadians now. Look across the train tracks into Ville LaSalle. Do you see how much land there is? The roads aren't even paved there. There's lots of work needed. I'm going to build a city, Maria.

MARIA: You better get back to the train station. (*exits*)

ROMANO: I won't be too long.

> *CENZO enters the yard. He is a strong, dark, charismatic man of 32 years. He carries a duffel bag. He looks around the yard to see if anyone has noticed him. ROMANO, sensing a presence, slowly turns to face him.*

ROMANO: Cenzo!

> *The men embrace and kiss each other on the cheeks Italian style.*

CENZO: My brother.

ROMANO: My sweet, sweet brother! I was worried. (*he embraces him again*) My God, I'm so happy to see you. It's been very lonely here. I mean...with Maria...it's fine...but we need more family.

CENZO: I'm here now. I'm here.

ROMANO: Look at you. You're still the actor type.

CENZO: Pe'la madonna, give me a poem, and I'll act circles around anyone. How are you?

ROMANO: Things are going well. I set up a company. Just like we dreamt of in Italy. Dicenzo Construction Company.

CENZO: You named it after our family. That's good.

ROMANO: I hire men based on the job. I usually work with these two guys, Pierre and Jacques. They work hard. Occasionally I hire Bruno. What I don't have is a master carpenter. We'll do better now that you're here. You don't know how much this means to me.

CENZO: You're the first of our family to come here. You've made it possible for all of us.

ROMANO: If it wasn't me it would've been you. How's our father?

CENZO: He's well. He told me to give you this. (*gives him a locket on a chain*)

ROMANO: (*opens the locket*) My mother, my sweet sweet mother. (*kisses the locket*) Pa is he…is he….

CENZO: Just last month, we both went to put flowers on her grave. Hey, don't worry about our father, he's got the strength of a Roman Legion.

> *MARIA enters the yard, she's put her hair up. She runs into CENZO's arms.*

MARIA: Cenzo, you're here! I was so scared, I thought you fell off the boat or something.

CENZO: (*overlapping*) Maria! Let me look at you. Nothing has changed. You're as beautiful as ever. (*they kiss on the cheeks*) I always told my brother, I said: "Roma' if you don't snap up Maria, somebody else will, and then you are going to die of a broken heart."

MARIA: Will you stop. Still the master actor you.

CENZO: And why not? I saw this picture of Clark Gable in a bar in Rome, I looked at it and I said: Pe'la madonna, is he a good looking man.

MARIA: You're better looking.

CENZO: True. But me, I'm thinking if this man can conquer the women of the world, then what can I do? I'll set them on fire.

MARIA: So you're not married yet?

CENZO: In my heart, I'm married. But when I wake up in the morning, my body tells me a different story. What do you want me to say? I eat, I dream, parrabee-parraba-parraboo, my life moves forward. Here. I have something. (*he takes out a package from his duffel bag wrapped in newspaper*) Home-made cheese.

MARIA: I miss this smell. We'll have some before dinner. I'll get the water boiling. (*exits*)

ROMANO: Cenzo, listen, let's not talk about business in front of Maria, she worries. (*pause*) I made a deal on five acres of land. It will be approved by the city at the end of the month.

CENZO: Where did you get the money?

ROMANO: What do you think I've been doing here all these years?

CENZO: I'd worry too. These are not the right times to be making such deals.

ROMANO: Will you stop with that small town mentality. Money is floating all over this city.

CENZO: Things don't look good, Romano. They just don't look good. There are reports, rumours, everyone is talking about it. Mussolini is going to enter the war on Germany's side.

ROMANO: That's impossible.

CENZO: Listen to me: The whole world is waiting to see what this man is going to do. What was the purpose of signing the pact with Germany? That makes him a partner. Do you understand? England and Germany are already at war. They're killing each other.

ROMANO: We're safe here.

CENZO: We're not safe. No one is. Tell me, do you know if they've arrested any Germans here in this country? (*pause*) Read this. (*he takes out a crumpled up newspaper article from his coat pocket, ROMANO reads the article*) These are regular citizens that have been arrested because their motherland is at war with Great Britain.

ROMANO: What are you saying?

CENZO: If Mussolini plunges Italy into war with England, this would make Italy an enemy of Canada. Do you understand? When Italy declares war, they will come after all of us here. It's only natural. Prepare for this. Because it's coming.

ROMANO: Mussolini is not stupid. He knows the Italians don't want to fight.

CENZO: He has no choice. My God, Hitler calls him Maestro. The man copied everything Mussolini created: intimidation tactics, controlling the newspapers, everything. But Germany has one thing Italy does not have.

ROMANO: What's that?

CENZO: The Germans are organized. They mean business. And the more they move forward, the worse it looks on Mussolini. He can't sit by while Germany collects all the countries of Europe.

ROMANO: That's why Mussolini is going to help the English. And the French.

CENZO: These are angry men. They have something to prove.

ROMANO: (*pause*) You saw me at the train station didn't you?

CENZO: Yes I did. I had your address. I walked from the station. I didn't want the authorities to know that you have an Italian in your home. In case you're being watched. They have lists—people of suspicious conduct. I'm trying to protect you.

ROMANO: Cenzo, Cenzo, you are still your old self. You go off exaggerating.

CENZO: On the ship there were some Jews who came from the north. I looked deep into their eyes as I heard their stories. Some had family in Poland, some in Germany, others in Croatia. These were doctors, merchants, and men of literature. These were bright minds. On the other side of the ship, I saw the rest of the Italians, regular workers like you and me. They all had this hope in their eyes, they were coming to meet cousins and sisters, some like me came to meet their brothers. They thought nothing of what was around them. To them it mattered only that they were leaving Italy and coming to America. Paradise. But when I looked at the Jews, they told different stories. Just before the war, these were respected people, now people were pointing fingers at them. They spoke of their families in Germany: they had their store windows smashed, others had their homes burnt down. People were boycotting their businesses. This is not an exaggeration. Yes they had hope in their hearts, but their eyes showed fear.

ROMANO: I was afraid too when I came here. But I've had some success. This is a decent and understanding country. Back in Italy, could we have started a construction company and earned a decent living?

CENZO: No.

ROMANO: In about a year, if I keep getting the work I'm getting, Dicenzo Construction will be an empire. Who would've thought of that just five years ago?

CENZO: You can't hide behind your work anymore. The world is at war, you are being forced to take a position. Why do you insist on ignoring this?

ROMANO: Cenzo, nobody is stopping us from moving forward here. This is a young country. They need us.

CENZO: They'll spit on you!

ROMANO: Stop it! Who do you think you are coming into my home talking like this! I've worked like a dog to give my life some hope, some direction. Maria slaves over a sewing machine making boring dresses for people to wear, and there are no complaints. That's what's good here. People don't go to war because of a complaint they have. They have the law here. And it's respected. You see this. (*takes out his citizenship papers from his coat pocket*) This says I am a Canadian. And as a Canadian I am entitled to all the rights and privileges provided by the law of the land. You have to think differently here, Cenzo. We keep our Italian ways in a cultural sense, but the rest, I left it on the boat. I threw it into the ocean. I said, if my country will not allow me to become a man and to live a life with honour and respect, then I will go elsewhere. This country here opened its arms, and gave me a chance. These people are not my enemies.

There is an awkward pause between the two men.
CENZO lights up a cigarette.

CENZO: We should not be fighting. I'm tired, Romano.

ROMANO: How stupid of me. Come in. Take your coat off. Wash up, relax. We're going to eat. A nice plate of pasta. (*calls off*) Maria, get Cenzo some wine!

CENZO: (*he suddenly grabs ROMANO and holds on to his head, forcing him to look into his eyes*) Look at me. I love you like you were my own child. You must promise me something.

ROMANO: Anything, anything. What?

CENZO: Does anybody know I'm here?

ROMANO: Except for Maria and Bruno, only Hélène knows.

CENZO: Who is she?

ROMANO: She's my neighbour.

CENZO: Do you trust her?

ROMANO: Why?

CENZO: Do you trust her?

ROMANO: Yes.

CENZO: Have you ever been inside her home?

ROMANO: What?

CENZO: You heard me.

ROMANO: She's usually here.

CENZO: You've never been inside her home?

ROMANO: No.

CENZO: This is your neighbour. Back in Italy we all knew what the inside of everyone else's home looked like. And yet you tell me you trust her. You tell no one that I'm here. No one.

ROMANO: Why?

CENZO: I'm not staying with you.

ROMANO: What?

CENZO: I'm not staying with you. I have an address for a boarding house. I'll stay there.

ROMANO: Why?

CENZO: In case something happens.

ROMANO: But Maria prepared a room just for you.

CENZO: Will you at least respect this much of what I'm saying?

ROMANO: Yes.

CENZO: We'll let some time go by. And then if you're right, I'll move in with you. Do you agree with this?

ROMANO: I don't feel good about it, but yes.

CENZO: Then there's one other thing. How much money do you have in the bank? Don't tell me. Tomorrow you go to the bank, you leave in your account two hundred dollars. The rest you take it out.

ROMANO: Cenzo....

CENZO: (*holding on to him even stronger, he cries slightly*) Don't you know that I love you. I'm your brother. Take your money out. Tell only Maria where you'll hide it. Don't even tell me. Do you understand? (*pause*) Do you understand?

ROMANO: Yes.

CENZO: (*pause, CENZO lets him go*) Good. Well. I'm getting hungry.

ROMANO: Cenzo. (*he motions for CENZO to come towards him, out of Maria's eyesight*) You must promise me something as well.

CENZO: Anything. I'll give you my life.

ROMANO: Should we be separated— (*pause*) Should we be separated. Promise me you'll look after her. If they do take me, promise me you'll look after her.

CENZO: Of course I will.

ROMANO: I don't know what I would do without her.

CENZO: She'll be fine. (*pause*) If they take me....

ROMANO: Cenzo....

CENZO: If they take me, you must deny that you even know me. Do you understand? I don't have the benefit of being a citizen. They'll think you're associating with a criminal. To them, we'll all be labelled Fascists.

MARIA enters with HÉLÈNE.

MARIA: Look who's back.

ROMANO: Hélène, come meet my brother. Cenzo, this is Hélène Beauchamp, our very dear friend and neighbour.

CENZO: (*takes her hand*) Enchanté.

HÉLÈNE: Vous parlez français?

CENZO: Un petit peu, oui.

HÉLÈNE: Je suis très heureuse de faire votre connaisance.

CENZO: C'est mon plaisir. Is this one of Maria's dresses?

HÉLÈNE: She just made it.

CENZO: In it you have the elegance of a ballerina.

HÉLÈNE: A ballerina?

CENZO: Paradise is filled with angels. They never talked about ballerinas.

HÉLÈNE: Voyons donc!
[Oh, please!]

ROMANO: With Maria's dresses, everybody looks good.

MARIA: Hélène is naturally beautiful, she doesn't need my dresses to make her look good.

CENZO: No...no, that's not what he's saying. But it adds something. A certain. Rhythm. One compliments the other. The lady the dress, the dress the lady.

HÉLÈNE: Les Italiens! Let me help you set the table.
(*exits*)

MARIA crosses to the edge of the door, and turns back.

MARIA: Cenzo. Did Romano tell you? We're having a baby.

This is not good news for CENZO. The thought that a child will be in the middle of impending turmoil does not sound good at all. He looks over towards ROMANO.

CENZO: (*he now looks at both of them, and begins to cry*) This is good news. This is the most beautiful news.

As the lights fade, we hear the news over the sound system.

RADIO ANNOUNCER: We interrupt our broadcast with this special bulletin: June 10, 1940. Italian Dictator Benito Mussolini has just declared war on England and France. Immediately upon hearing the news, Prime Minister Mackenzie King declared war on Italy. Asked what would happen to suspected Italians here in Canada, he would not give an answer, but said that plans are now being mobilized to protect the citizens of this country. A few days ago, President Roosevelt gave a speech which many interpreted as a final warning to Mussolini. Said the President: "The war has just doubled in size." When asked to comment, he did not give any indications on what would happen to citizens of Italian descent. Meanwhile in Germany, Hitler was all smiles when hearing of the Italian Dictator's actions....

Scene 2

It is now early evening of June 10, 1940. MARIA and HÉLÈNE appear in the backyard. BRUNO runs in.

MARIA: Did you find him?

BRUNO: No. He could be anywhere.

HÉLÈNE: Maria, you're getting all worked up for nothing.

BRUNO: I still don't believe it. I never thought Mussolini would enter the war. Even the Fascists in the city didn't think he'd do it. (*pause*) Now that Italy is in the war, one thing is for sure.

HÉLÈNE: What's that?

BRUNO: The Germans will eat well. (*pause*)

ROMANO enters the yard.

MARIA: Romano. (*she hugs him*) Did you hear?

ROMANO: Hear what?

BRUNO: Where have you been?

ROMANO: With my lawyer. I've been on the road all day. Why?

MARIA: Mussolini declared war on England.

ROMANO: (*pause*) Where's Cenzo?

MARIA: We thought he was with you.

ROMANO: No. He's finishing up the work on the other site. Hélène, here's some money. Run to the store and bring back some groceries.

HÉLÈNE: What do you need?

ROMANO: Anything, just use up the money. Please.

HÉLÈNE: Okay. Maria, I'll be back. (*exits*)

We hear MARIA's name being shouted from the house.

MARIA: That's Teresina. I'll go see what she wants. (*exits*)

BRUNO: Be on guard, Romano, I'm speaking objectively here. You're a man of high profile. People know you. Be careful how you do business.

ROMANO: You're not wearing your black shirt today?

BRUNO: It makes no difference what you think of me. I'll still be the uncle of your child. (*ROMANO walks away*) Listen to me. My advice to you is to cease operation of your business. Just for a little while. Your brother is not a citizen. He's been here just a month. They could consider him a spy, an organizer of underground activity. Stay away from him.

ROMANO: He's my brother.

BRUNO: Think of Maria. It makes no difference if Cenzo is the Pope himself. It matters only that he's an Italian with no citizenship papers. Do you understand the implications of that?

ROMANO: Who have you been talking to?

BRUNO: Damn it, Romano, they're watching you!

CENZO enters the yard.

CENZO: Get out of here now! The authorities are all over the place. They've blocked the bridges. They're coming. Romano, let's go.

ROMANO: I'm staying with Maria.

BRUNO: What are you talking about?

CENZO: The arrests.

MARIA enters the yard.

MARIA: Teresina can't find her son. He should've been home by now.

BRUNO: (*overlapping*) What arrests?

CENZO: They're not in the neighbourhood yet, so there's still time.

MARIA: Time for what? Time for what?

ROMANO: (*overlapping*) What did Teresina say?

MARIA: She can't find her son.

CENZO: They're rounding us up as we speak!

ROMANO: Everybody listen to me! We won't achieve a thing with all these nerves. Nothing. We go on as usual. What else can we do?

CENZO: Things have changed. The rules are different now.

BRUNO: I know a Justice of the Peace of Italian descent. Things should be okay.

CENZO: Mussolini has just launched us all in a war whether we like it or not!

BRUNO: Wait a minute here, I'm a Canadian Citizen, I pay my taxes.

CENZO: You're a fool, Ciccio. Mussolini just kissed your citizenship goodbye. As of today, Canada is an enemy of Italy. Today, while we were working, and heard the news, Pierre and Jacques walked off the job. Now they're scared of Italians. If it was up to me, I'd fire those fuckers!

ROMANO: We can't just suddenly make these decisions.

BRUNO: You don't just fire people for being scared.

CENZO: Stay out of this....

ROMANO: He's right....

BRUNO: Those men are unionized workers, there are rules.

CENZO: Hey, Ciccio, what are you, a fucking captain all of a sudden?

BRUNO: I know the law. If you were around more, you'd learn.

CENZO: Look, Ciccio, I don't need your advice on how to run a business.

BRUNO: Stop calling me Ciccio. You call me Bruno or don't call me at all!

> *CENZO suddenly moves towards BRUNO as if ready to take him on.*

MARIA: Listen to me all of you! Cenzo! (*he stops dead in his tracks*) Bruno, go home to Rita. She'll need you there. Bruno.

> *BRUNO exits.*

ROMANO: (*MARIA staggers slightly*) Maria, what is it? Sit down.

MARIA: It's nothing...it's the heat.... (*feels her stomach*) It's okay.

HÉLÈNE enters the yard.

HÉLÈNE: There's policemen all over the place…. I don't know what to do. Cenzo….

ROMANO: Hélène, listen to me, take Maria inside. Just do as I say! (*HÉLÈNE crosses to MARIA. He looks at his brother. There is no choice in the matter. ROMANO has to stay with his wife.*) Maria, it's going to be okay.

HÉLÈNE: What do you want me to do?

> *While ROMANO is talking to HÉLÈNE and MARIA, CENZO has succeeded in running behind them and running in the direction of HÉLÈNE's house. He exits.*

ROMANO: Promise me you'll take care of her?

HÉLÈNE: What have you done?

ROMANO: JUST PROMISE ME!

HÉLÈNE: Yes, yes, I will!

> *An RCMP officer has quietly entered from the house.*

RCMP OFFICER 1: Romano Dicenzo!

MARIA: (*abruptly*) What is it you want?

> *Another RCMP officer has entered the yard. ROMANO runs towards MARIA.*

RCMP OFFICER 2: No one out front, Chief!

MARIA: What do you want with us?

RCMP OFFICER 2: (*shouting off*) Okay, guys we got someone out back here!

ROMANO: What do you want with me?

RCMP OFFICER 1: Are you Romano Dicenzo?

ROMANO: Who are you?

RCMP OFFICER 1: Are you Romano Dicenzo?

ROMANO: Yes I am.

RCMP OFFICER 1: RCMP. I have here a warrant for your arrest. Cuff him.

MARIA: Leave him alone! He's done nothing wrong!

RCMP OFFICER 1: And you are?

MARIA: I'm his wife.

RCMP OFFICER 1: Your name?

MARIA: Maria.

RCMP OFFICER 1: Is she on the list?

RCMP OFFICER 2: (*checks the list*) No, captain.

RCMP OFFICER 1: Then it would serve you well to not interfere with police business.

HÉLÈNE: Qu'est-ce que vous faites ici?
[What are you doing?]

RCMP OFFICER 1: (*to his partner*) Hey, Michel! Come talk to this lady!

RCMP OFFICER 2: Mademoiselle, s'il vous plait, ça ne vous regarde pas. Rentrez chez vous.
[Please lady, this doesn't concern you. Go home.]

ROMANO: I'm a Canadian citizen!

RCMP OFFICER 1: You're Italian.

RCMP OFFICER 2: Captain, I found this inside. (*hands him the papers*) Probably some Fascist propaganda!

RCMP OFFICER 1: (*holding up an Italian newspaper featuring Benito Mussolini on the cover*) Yes. Here he is. Il Duce. Do you inspire your fellow Italians with this?

MARIA: It's just a newspaper! It's all we have to read.

RCMP OFFICER 1: Then you know your Duce just declared war on England.

ROMANO: What have I done?

RCMP OFFICER 1: Under the Defence Of Canada Regulations, you are being arrested on suspicion of subversive actions. You are Italian. You are now our enemy. We are at war!

ROMANO: Where are you taking me?

RCMP OFFICER 1: Lock him up with the others!

HÉLÈNE: (*moving towards him*) You can at least tell the man where you're taking him.

RCMP OFFICER 2: Ce n'est pas de vos affaires!
[It's none of your business!]

RCMP OFFICER 1: I warn you, do not interfere with police business.

MARIA: They can't do this! We have rights!

RCMP OFFICER 1: Your rights were suspended the minute you declared war on this great nation. (*he finds a photograph in amongst the papers*) Who is this?

ROMANO: It's a picture.

RCMP OFFICER 1: I can see it's a picture, my man. I asked who is this at your side? (*pause*) I hate repeating myself. Who is this man? (*pause*) Very well then. (*crosses to HÉLÈNE*) Have you seen this man before?

HÉLÈNE: (*she suddenly realizes that CENZO is gone*) I...I....

RCMP OFFICER 1: (*to ROMANO*) You see what you've just done? By not answering my question, you've forced me to implicate your neighbour here. If he's on the list and you don't tell us, this lady here will be arrested. Do you understand? For helping in subversive activities. (*turns to HÉLÈNE*) Have you seen this man?

ROMANO: That's a picture taken in Italy.

RCMP OFFICER 1: And his name? (*pause*) His name?

HÉLÈNE: That's his brother.

RCMP OFFICER 1: Is this true, Mademoiselle Beauchamp?

HÉLÈNE: How did you know my name?

RCMP OFFICER 1: Now. I need his name.

HÉLÈNE: Cenzo. His name is Cenzo.

RCMP OFFICER 1: Where is he?

MARIA: He doesn't live here.

RCMP OFFICER 1: Where is he, ma'am?

HÉLÈNE: She's telling you the truth, he doesn't live here.

RCMP OFFICER 1: Stay away from these people. They'll just cause you trouble.

RCMP OFFICER 2: There's no Cenzo on the list, sir.

RCMP OFFICER 1: (*to HÉLÈNE*) We know everything there is to know! We are at war! Italians are dangerous people! They are Fascists! They're here to hurt us! Do you understand! Turn them in! It is your only choice! They are not to be trusted! They are now your enemies! (*to MARIA*) Would you like to say goodbye to your husband?

MARIA: Romano....

RCMP OFFICER 1: That's good. Take him away!

ROMANO is escorted away.

ROMANO: (*offstage*) Maria, you just stay calm. I'll be back. You hear me! I'll be back!

MARIA: Romano! Romano! He hasn't done anything! He hasn't done anything!

HÉLÈNE: Maria. Please. Go inside!

RCMP OFFICER 2: (*offstage*) That's ten men, sir. There should be another five men just on this block!

HÉLÈNE: What's going to happen to him?

RCMP OFFICER 1: The world is at war. You should concern yourself with more important things. (*crosses to MARIA*) See how many friends you have now? (*exits*)

> *MARIA gathers her strength. There is an awkward pause between the two women.*

HÉLÈNE: I'm sorry.... I.... you heard the man. They're watching us. Where did he go? Where did Cenzo go? Maria. Listen to what these men say. Romano will be back, you'll see. He'll be back. I'm sorry.... I'm sorry. I have to go to my father. (*exits*)

> *MARIA looks up towards the sky as if searching for an answer. We hear the sounds of the vehicles screeching away and the sirens sounding. As the lights fade we hear a news bulletin over the sound system.*

RADIO ANNOUNCER: In response to Italy's declaration of war, Prime Minister Mackenzie King put into effect the War Measures Act. Six thousand Italian men have been arrested for suspicion of subversive acts. Officially they are to be labelled "Enemy Aliens." With this mobilization, the Prime Minister is guaranteeing the safety of the country. All citizens are asked to help with the war effort. Should you know of any suspicious characters, you are to report them to your local police station or

RCMP office immediately. As for the Italians, those who have not been arrested must report once a month to the RCMP. This is the law....

Scene 3

Later that night. A Montréal POLICE OFFICER appears at a desk. Bordeaux Jail, Montréal.

POLICE OFFICER: Next! *(ROMANO enters)* You are?

ROMANO: Romano Dicenzo.

POLICE OFFICER: (*checks his list*) Yes. (*he writes on the list*) You are now Prisoner Number 432. (*he writes all pertinent information on a slate*) Hold this up, son. (*hands the slate to ROMANO, who holds it up near his face*) Stand back a bit. (*Pause. ROMANO does not move. He goes up to him.*) What part of Italy you from?

ROMANO: Campobasso.

POLICE OFFICER: You're cut off from the sea there, aren't you?

ROMANO: It's all mountains and hills. Nothing more.

POLICE OFFICER: Yes. Now, son, just stand back a little won't you? (*ROMANO does so*) There you go. (*the photo is snapped*)

ROMANO: Where am I?

POLICE OFFICER: You're at the Bordeaux Jail, son. You won't be here for long.

ROMANO: Will I be going home?

POLICE OFFICER: No, son. (*he escorts ROMANO off*) Next!

Scene 4

A day later. MARIA appears anxiously waiting on a street outside a grocery store. BRUNO enters.

BRUNO: Have you been in yet?

MARIA: He won't let me in. I can't get into Lorenzo's, there's a whole mob in front of his store.

The STORE OWNER comes out holding a broom.

STORE OWNER: What do you people want?

MARIA: I want to buy some bread.

STORE OWNER: We're all out.

BRUNO: Come on, I see a whole shelf full of bread.

STORE OWNER: Look, mister, you best get on out of here. We're not selling to no Italians.

BRUNO: (*moves towards him*) But, sir....

STORE OWNER: (*holds his broom up*) I'm not telling you again.

MARIA: We have money.

STORE OWNER: Your money isn't good here. Now get out of here!

We hear a window crashing offstage. We hear people shouting and some cursing in Italian.

MARIA: What is going on?

STORE OWNER: See what you people started.

BRUNO: Come on, let's just go home.

LORENZO rushes in.

MARIA: Lorenzo, cosa fanno al tuo negozio?
[Lorenzo, what are they doing to your store?]

LORENZO: Disgraziati! Sta gente sono propio animali! Pe tri anni n'daiu stu storu, e mo ti tratanu comu na bestia!

[Bastards! These people are real animals! Three years I've had this store, and now they treat me like a dog!]

STORE OWNER: I'm giving you all one more minute, and I'm going to call the cops!

LORENZO: Hey, missyou,tu po ghieri a fanculu tu e la puttana di mammata, pecchi l'unglese non lu capiscu.

[Hey, mister, you can go fuck yourself, you and that whore of your mother, because I don't understand English.]

STORE OWNER: English, English, Lorenzo, start talking English!

LORENZO: Missyou, h'aio niente a fare cu tia, va bene!

[Mister, I have nothing to do with you, understand!]

STORE OWNER: You Fascist prick! (*raises his broom*)

LORENZO: Mina, mina, brutto, schifossu!

[Go for it, go for it, you disgusting ingrate!]

BRUNO: (*intervening*) Lorenzo, calmati! Come on, sir. Let it go. He's just afraid. Look at what they're doing to his store.

STORE OWNER: That's not my problem. Now this is my final warning. Don't ever show your faces here again.

LORENZO: Che sta dicendo chisto? Why you me no like no more? Che ti ho fatto?

[What's he saying? Why don't you like me anymore? What have I done to you?]

STORE OWNER: English, you stupid fucking wop! English!

LORENZO: Me no speak no eenglish. I speak francese, va bene. Disgraziato!
[I don't speak English. I speak French, alright. You disgraceful ingrate!]

STORE OWNER: That's it, I've had it. Police! (*exits*)

BRUNO: Come on, lets get out of here.

LORENZO: Io sunnu Calabrese, io nu scapu, va bene.
[I'm a Calabrese, I don't run, alright.]

BRUNO: Lorenzo, non ci sta niente da fare, andiamo.
[Lorenzo, there is nothing to do here, let's go.]

LORENZO: Ció tre guagliuni, come faccio? Guarda'mu storu! (*he breaks down*) Guardu, guardu. Come faccio? Bastardi!
[I have three children, what'll I do? Look at my store! What'll I do? Bastards!]

MARIA: Hold him by the hand. Let's go. (*they exit*)

> *We hear more shouting: "There he is!" "Run you Fascist pig!" We hear more windows crashing. We hear a police whistle: "Police! Stop!" The STORE OWNER enters.*

STORE OWNER: Police! This way! I need some security! This is a fucking war here!

Scene 5

> *The next day. An RCMP office. MARIA appears standing in front of an RCMP OFFICER at a desk.*

RCMP OFFICER: Your name?

MARIA: Maria Dicenzo.

RCMP OFFICER: Step forward. (*she does so*) We need your fingerprints. (*he motions to her*) Now, stand back. (*she does so*) Hold still. (*he snaps a photo*) Now:

You don't leave the city without our permission. You are to report to us once a month and tell us of your activities. Your salary has been suspended. As have your rights and privileges as a Canadian citizen. On your monthly visit, you will be given $12.00. Do you understand this?

MARIA: Why is this….

RCMP OFFICER: Just answer the question.

MARIA: Yes.

RCMP OFFICER: This is the law. Any breach of regulations, you will go to jail. Is that understood?

MARIA: Yes.

RCMP OFFICER: If you know of any Italian that has not registered with the RCMP, you will be in violation of the law. Do you understand these rules and regulations?

MARIA: Yes I do.

RCMP OFFICER: You can go home now.

Scene 6

HÉLÈNE and her father, a few hours later.

M. BEAUCHAMP: Hélène, écoute-moi bien. Tu as écouté les nouvelles. C'est la loi. Je ne veux plus que tu voies ces gens-là.
[Hélène, listen to me. You heard the news. It's the law. You stay away from these people.]

HÉLÈNE: Mais ce sont nos amis.
[But they're our friends.]

M. BEAUCHAMP: Et enlève cette robe. Ça va te causer des ennuies.
[And take off that dress. It could get you in trouble.]

HÉLÈNE: Ils n'ont rien fait du mal.
[They've done nothing wrong.]

M. BEAUCHAMP: Tu vas m'écouter! Je suis ton père et tu dois m'obéir. Si ta mère était encore avec nous, je n'aurais pas ce problème. On a aussi arrêté des Canadiens. Hélène, je veux te protéger. Tu vas travailler au magasin, et tu rentres à la maison tout de suite après. C'est compris, là? Dès que je trouve des nouveaux locataires, les Dicenzo ficherent le camp. Je suis obligé par la loi. Et toi aussi. C'est claire?
[Now you listen to me! I'm your father, and you better obey me! If your mother was still alive I wouldn't have this problem. They've arrested some French Canadian men as well. I'm doing this to protect you. You will work at the store, and come straight home. Is that understood? As soon as I find new tenants, I will evict the Dicenzos. I must obey the law. And so will you. Is that clear?]

HÉLÈNE: Oui, papa.
[Yes, papa.]

Scene 7

Early that evening. LORENZO appears at a street corner, examining the ruin of his grocery store.

LORENZO: Bastardi! Animali! Vigliaci! Mi posso schiatare lu iornu che sono venuto a stu paesi.
[Bastards! Animals! Cowards! I curse the day I set foot in this country.]

Two men enter. They approach Lorenzo quietly.

MAN 2: Lorenzo.

LORENZO: Wey, Peppino. Chi si dice? Guarda. Su civili sta gente?
[Hey, Peppino. What do you say? Look. You call these people civil?]

MAN 1: What's he saying?

MAN 2: His store is fucked up.

LORENZO: Che facete a quest'ora?
[What are you doing at this hour?]

MAN 1: Go ahead, ask him.

MAN 2: Cerchiamo un uomo che si chiama Cenzo Dicenzo? Lo conosci?
[We're looking for a man named Cenzo Dicenzo? Do you know him?]

LORENZO: Mboh!

MAN 1: Don't give me that fucking shit! We're looking for Cenzo. Now where is he?

LORENZO: Hey, missyou. Ma che volete da me?
[Hey, mister. What do you want from me?]

MAN 1: I don't understand your fucking language.

MAN 2: Take it easy!

MAN 1: This time it was your store. Next time it's your home. You tell us where Cenzo is, and you'll be fine.

LORENZO: Cha detto?
[What did he say?]

MAN 2: La prossima volta stu cassino te lo fanno a casa tua.
[The next time, this mess will be done at your house.]

LORENZO: (*goes for MAN 1*) Ma io t'amazzu! (*MAN 2 intervenes*) Ti scash a testa e ti d'assu cha la strada per quindici iorni.

[I'll kill you! I'll break your head and leave your lying in the street for fifteen days.]

MAN 2: Lorenzo, calmati.

[Lorenzo, calm down.]

MAN 1: (*overlapping*) You want to be a hero, you stupid guinea wop! You stay out of buying a home from Dicenzo Construction, you understand?

LORENZO: Hey, missyou, who make you come to talk to me?

MAN 1: Guido Lombardo.

MAN 2: Hai capito come vanno le cose? Guido Lombardo.

[You understand how things work now? Guido Lombardo.]

MAN 1: You find us Cenzo. And you'll be okay. (*they exit*)

LORENZO: Guido Lombardo. Figlio di puttana!

[Guido Lombardo. Son of a whore!]

Scene 8

Later that night. The backyard. MARIA is sitting on the steps. BRUNO enters.

BRUNO: Do you have food for tonight? (*pause*) I've asked everyone. I've been to the Office of Immigration, the police, everyone. Even the newspapers won't tell you. It's war. The rules change. Based on what they must be thinking, it has everything to do with security reasons. Once they're properly organized, they'll let you know. They have to. The world is watching. You be careful who you talk to. This isn't over yet.

LORENZO enters the yard. He is lost in thought, oblivious of their presence.

MARIA: Lorenzo. (*pause*) Lorenzo, parlami.
[Lorenzo. Lorenzo, talk to me.]

LORENZO: (*pause*) Mi hanno ruvinatu lu storu. Mi hanno rubatto il mio figlio.
[They've ruined my store. They've stolen my son.]

BRUNO: They took his son, I don't believe it.

LORENZO: Stu mundo e finitu. Non ci sta chiu a giustizia. Fam'andare a Teresina, non credo che la passa buona. (*exits*)
[This world is finished. There is no more justice. Let me go check on Teresina, I don't think she's doing well.]

BRUNO: Coraggio, Lorenzo, coraggio.
[Courage, Lorenzo, courage.]

CENZO enters in the yard.

MARIA: Cenzo! My God! Where have you been? Do you know where Romano is?

CENZO: I've been hiding. Are you okay? (*pause*) Most probably Romano is in a war camp. Anyone who is regarded with suspicion will be brought there. Last night, I heard some men talking: over six thousand have been arrested. This all in two days. They had this planned. There is no way the authorities could've been that efficient without some help. There are informers around us.

BRUNO: What are you talking about?

CENZO: I'm talking about informers! People who've been approached to give names. It could be anyone. Including Italians. Just to save their own

skin, they will point a finger at someone. (*pause*)
Did Romano ever attend any meetings with Fascists?

MARIA: He hates the Fascists. That's why he came to
Canada. They're all a bunch of hypocrites!

CENZO: Let's not talk of hypocrisy! At least in Italy, you
know who your enemies are. Here, they all have the
same face, both friend and enemy alike!

MARIA: Why weren't the two of you arrested?

CENZO: We don't count. We're not important to them.
You see, Romano is an employer of men. He creates
work. You cut him off from the community, the
Italians are weaker.

BRUNO: You have to register with the RCMP. We have
to report to them once a month. They want to know
where we've been, what we're doing, everything.
They've suspended our salaries. They'll give us
$12.00 a month to live with. There's no way to beat
this.

CENZO: I still have the company. I'll continue to work.
I have the two trucks.

BRUNO: You have nothing! Do you understand?

MARIA: They took the trucks away.

CENZO: Who did?

MARIA: The government, the authorities...they....
(*hands him a letter*) The Custodian Of Alien
Property. They seized everything Romano owned.
The trucks, the equipment, everything. They will
sell it. (*pause*) They took everything. We have
nothing.

CENZO: Does Romano's lawyer know about this?

MARIA: I'll go see him.

CENZO: Alright. (*pause*) Do you have some money?

MARIA: Yes. Romano took care of it....

CENZO: Don't tell me. I know nothing. Understand? You know nothing of me. We'll meet at night. We should never be seen together. In case they think I'm dangerous, you'll be safe. Now, in case time goes by, and you don't hear from me, we will meet Friday nights at the church. We should be able to talk there. There's an informer somewhere in our neighbourhood. It could be anyone. Do you understand? Bruno, you have to help me. Just keep playing the village idiot. People ask you something, you don't know. Together we'll find this bastard!

BRUNO: You're telling me to spy on my friends.

CENZO: They're not your friends if they fingered Romano. (*pause*) Who were Romano's main competitors within the construction business?

BRUNO: Why?

CENZO: With Romano arrested, it ruins his company.

BRUNO: Romano ran a two truck operation. There is no threat there.

CENZO: His competitors could be recruiting workers as we speak.

BRUNO: Romano was careless, I'm telling you.

CENZO: Don't you judge my brother.

BRUNO: I'm not, I'm just...look, don't take it out on me! Alright! I'm not the one who goes whoring around with a French woman. That is not the mark of an honourable man. You could show some caution. You fuck around with a French woman, and Maria here is a witness to her disgrace, what position does that put her in? You make one mistake with Hélène, she goes straight to the authorities claiming she's been victimized by an

Italian who happens to be your husband's brother. They'll come after you too!

CENZO: You don't know anything about me and Hélène.

BRUNO: Hey, paesa', you have no citizenship papers, you understand? You're the first one they'll come after.

HÉLÈNE enters the yard carrying two bags of food.

HÉLÈNE: (*pause*) What are you doing here? You should not be here. Did he tell you what he did? Tell her. You were hiding in my home! If the police found out you could've gotten my family in trouble! You had no right to hide in my father's house!…the newspapers, the radio…they're telling us to stay away from the Italians. That parade you Italians had last month. People talking of Mussolini. The Sons Of Italy shouting the greatness of il Duce….

BRUNO: That was not The Sons Of Italy. We were there for St. Anthony.

HÉLÈNE: …but the Fascists were there.

BRUNO: St. Anthony does not discriminate.

HÉLÈNE: You watched this! I saw you. If the Fascists were bad people, why did you watch?

MARIA: You were watching too. Does that make you a bad person?

HÉLÈNE: I have the right to watch! I was born here, I'm four generations of the Family Beauchamp. You heard what the RCMP said. I've never been talked to that way in my life. He asked you for his name, why didn't you respond? Why was I put into that position? Why? If you're all guilty of something, I must report you. That is the law.

48

CENZO: Maria has done nothing wrong. Look. (*he takes out a piece of paper*) This is where I sleep. It's a boarding house. You want me arrested, I'll be there. (*pause*) I've been here a month. And already I've seen a lot. You may have been here four generations, and you French people might be more in number, but why do the English have all the bigger homes? Why do the English run all the big businesses? Why do the English not speak French, while you French people speak English? Why do they want us to fight? We share the same language you and I. Italian and French are brothers and sisters in terms of language. And now the English are telling you to hate us, why? You mean to tell me that after four generations of the Beauchamp family all you can show for it is a grocery store? Who is your enemy, Hélène? Who? (*pause*) You can't tell me to my face that you French people have not spoken of the English in this way? Can you? (*pause*) I thought so. So take my address and point a finger at me. You'll just be playing their game.

MARIA: (*pause*) This night air is not good for me.

HÉLÈNE: My friends don't talk to me anymore. I have my father to look after. He's old.

MARIA: Then you should look after him. You do what is right for you.

HÉLÈNE: They're telling me not even to talk to you!

MARIA: Then you shouldn't.

HÉLÈNE: I just want you to understand the situation. Things must carry on. As before. Do you understand? (*pause*) Maria. You pay my father rent, and we've been good to you.

MARIA: Yes.

HÉLÈNE: The rent still has to be paid.

MARIA: I know.

HÉLÈNE: How will you do it? (*pause*) And when the baby is born, who will look after it?

MARIA: Teresina will help me. I have my cousin here. You came here for the rent?

HÉLÈNE: Yes.

MARIA: I was expecting it. (*she hands HÉLÈNE the rent money*)

HÉLÈNE: Do you have some food? (*offers her one of the bags*) Take this. I don't need it. (*pause*) Don't be stubborn. Take it.

MARIA: (*pause*) No.

HÉLÈNE: Maria, please.

MARIA: (*pause*) No. I'll be fine.

HÉLÈNE: I'll leave the food by my back door. It will be there if you want it. Just take it. (*pause*) Do you know where your husband is?

MARIA: No.

HÉLÈNE: You'll hear soon enough. (*pause*) Good night.

MARIA: Yes. (*MARIA and BRUNO exit*)

CENZO: Who just spoke right now? That's not you talking. Who is it, your father? Your friends? Who's telling you to hate us?

HÉLÈNE: You heard the news.

CENZO: Can you put a face to it?

HÉLÈNE: We have to live too, you know!

CENZO: I'm not talking about the rent! What more do you want from Maria? Can't you see that she's helpless. What has she done? In plain simple language. Tell me. (*pause*) This dress you're wearing, didn't Maria make it for you? You wear her clothes, you don't need to treat her this way. (*pause*) This whole month meant nothing to you?

HÉLÈNE: Let's just stay away from each other. It's the law. It's different now. We can't be seen together, do you understand? Go away.

CENZO: Is this what you want? No one knows we're here. If you truly felt I was dangerous, you would've turned me in already. You knew I was going to be here tonight. You came. Why are you still talking to me? Come on, I'll walk you to the RCMP office right now. Let's get this over with.

HÉLÈNE: Please....

CENZO: We're just two people coming together. What's wrong with that? You felt nothing? Just last week: the movie, drinks, dancing.... It could still be the same....

HÉLÈNE: No.

CENZO: Is this what you want? (*pause*) You wore your Italian dress for me, didn't you? Tonight you showed yourself. You knew I was going to be here.

HÉLÈNE: I don't know anything about you! Comprends-tu? Je te connais pas! Tu peux pas rentrer dans ma vie pis après un mois me parler de cette façon-là. Pour qui tu te prends? Comprends-tu ce que je dis? Who are you?
[Understand? I don't know you! You can't come into my life for a month and speak to me like that. Who do you think you are? Do you understand me?]

CENZO: The furthest thing from my mind is to put you in danger. I've been stripped of everything. My name, my history, my homeland, my family, I have no idea what they've done to my brother. And I stand here in your presence with just my word. (*pause, he shows her a pair of earrings*) These earrings were my mother's. They're all I have that bring me back to my past. I was going to give them to you. She wore them everyday of her life. Take them. I want nothing in return. If your safety means being away from you, then that's what I'll do. When I left my country I saw how bad things could be, when I met you I saw how good things could be. I gave it a chance. (*pause*) Sleep well.

HÉLÈNE: Cenzo. (*pause*) Cenzo. (*Pause. He goes to her. He touches her.*) I….

CENZO: Is this wrong? (*takes her hands*) …is this touch not what you expected?

HÉLÈNE: I might get in trouble.

CENZO: Who will know? (*he kisses her*)

HÉLÈNE: No. (*she kisses him*)

CENZO: Should I leave?

HÉLÈNE: No.

CENZO: I'll stay. (*he kisses her*)

HÉLÈNE: Stay.

CENZO: I will.

HÉLÈNE: Stay.

CENZO: I will.

> *They continue kissing, as the lights fade slowly to black.*

ACT TWO

Scene 1

September 16, 1940. Camp Petawawa. A Military Drum Cadence blares in the distance. LIEUTENANT-COLONEL ROBERT LUCERNE stands on an upper level in full view of the entire camp population. To his side is STAFF SERGEANT BILL DUNNISON. A Camp Guard armed with a sub-machine gun stands at attention.

LUCERNE: My name is Lieutenant-Colonel Robert Lucerne. You address me as sir. You are prisoners of war. This is a Prisoner of War Camp. You are our guests. So we are going to be nice to you. You are surrounded by over two hundred miles of deep, dark forest. To the north is the Ottawa River. You have no way of escaping. Should you try, you will be shot on sight. (*pause*) As our guests, you will respect our rules. The chain of command works thusly: each hut has elected a Barracks leader. There are twelve huts, so there are twelve leaders. These leaders have elected a Camp Spokesman by secret ballot. You, the leaders, are responsible for the cleanliness and orderly maintenance of your barracks. I will personally inspect each individual hut. You will represent the inhabitants of your hut to the Camp's Spokesman. The Camp Spokesman is the official intermediary between the internees and the military command. He will receive my orders given to him at meetings held twice a week. He will then transmit those orders to the other hut leaders. Breakfast is served between 0600 and 0700 hours. Lunch from 1145 to 1245 hours. Supper: 1700 to 1800 hours. You will be allowed to purchase items from the canteen. As all your possessions have been taken away, for currency, you will be given cardboard notes valued at five, ten, and twenty cents, and a dollar. This is the legal tender in the Camp. Once the roll has been called by the hut leader in the presence of the Sergeant, the barrack will be locked at 2100 hours. Lights go out at 2200 hours. Afterwards, speaking—even lighting up a cigarette is prohibited. (*pause*) We are in a state of war, gentlemen, and as such, all precautions will be taken with incoming mail. We have a Camp Censor who will inspect all the mail and parcels: magazines, newspapers, etc. Letters will be read by the censor. You have the right to write three letters per month of 24 lines, and four postcards, 8 lines in length. Staff Sergeant Dunnison here is well versed in over a dozen languages. That includes Italian. We will know everything. (*pause*) Within this camp you may have noticed there are Germans. In a few days they will all be shipped out. That will make you Italians the majority here. Don't think for a minute that it will make you the reigning power. Do you see these guards? Their guns are always loaded, and ready to fire. Should you need a demonstration, one can be provided for you. All I need is for one of you to make a run for it. (*pause*) Tomorrow you will be given your work details. (*pause*) Welcome to Camp Petawawa. (*turns to DUNNISON*) Dunnison, do you have the results of the vote?

DUNNISON: Yes I do. I have him waiting by your office, sir.

LUCERNE: How many Italians do we have here?

DUNNISON: Just over six hundred, sir.

LUCERNE: Precisely how many?

DUNNISON: I'll have to count the list, sir. I'll have the count by mid-morning.

> *They exit. ROMANO, LUCA, CALO, and VITO enter. They are clothed in grey-blue prison uniforms.*

CALO: If they don't kill us, the heat will. (*Pause. He picks up a pebble from the ground. He crosses to VITO.*) Turn around. (*We see a red circle on the back of the uniform; a bulls-eye. He gently tosses the pebble. He hits the target.*) It works. You want to see if mine works? I think we look like a bunch of clowns if you ask me.

LUCA: (*moves towards CALO*) You calling me a clown?

ROMANO: (*sensing a fight about to happen, he steps in*) Where you from?

CALO: Toronto. My name is Calo Calabrese, my family's from Catanzarro. I'm a musician.

ROMANO: I'm from Montréal. I'm originally from Campobasso. I'm in construction. What kind of music do you play?

CALO: I can play anything. The accordion, mandolin, guitar, horns.

ROMANO: That's good. (*he walks over to LUCA*) And you, where are you from?

LUCA: What's it to you?

ROMANO: We're going to be living in the same hut, we may as well get to know each other.

LUCA: You think you can just come up to me and ask questions? (*pause*) Mind your own business.

VITO starts coughing violently. ROMANO goes to him.

CALO: This guy needs a doctor.

ROMANO: You're shaking.

LUCA: (*crosses to VITO and hands him a bottle*) Here. Drink this. (*pause*) Trust me. (*VITO drinks, the coughing stops. LUCA touches his arm, he grimaces in pain.*) What happened?

VITO: It's nothing, a guard overreacted.

CALO: These guards are over-anxious. They're pushing us around. It's not right.

ROMANO: (*to VITO*) My name is Romano Dicenzo.

VITO: I'm Vito Di Napoli. I've heard of you, I've seen your trucks all over Montréal. Who's looking after the business?

ROMANO: My—My employees should do well. When we're all done here, you can come work with me. How old are you?

VITO: Eighteen.

CALO: They arrested even the young ones. What could they want with a young kid like this?

LUCA: You're ignorant. That's such an ignorant question.

CALO: Hey, paesa', we're just making small talk over here! I don't need your opinions!

LUCA: I've seen you before. You play with the Carini Band. (*pause*) Roberto Carini is the biggest Fascist in Toronto. He's caused us nothing but problems.

ROMANO: Are you a Fascist?

CALO: I told you, I'm a musician. And if I am a Fascist, what's wrong with that?

LUCA: I'd rather be a Communist than one of you Fascist pigs!

CALO: We know you're not a Communist, they put them all on the other side. You don't look like a righteous man, so what...you live by the knife?

LUCA crosses towards CALO, ROMANO stands in his way.

ROMANO: Leave him alone. Why are you doing this?

VITO: (*pause*) Did you meet the French prisoners from Quebec? They wouldn't fight in the army. Isn't that treason?

CALO: Of course it is.

LUCA: Here he is with his fucking opinions again.

CALO: What are you in for?

LUCA: (*moves towards CALO*) You keep your mouth shut!

VITO: Will you guys stop, you'll get us all shot

ROMANO and LUCA stand off, neither one wanting to give in. Finally LUCA moves away.

CALO: You can't reason with him.

VITO: (*pause*) Where are we?

CALO: It's nothing but woods. We're in the middle of a forest.

VITO: What will they do to us? I was fixing the door to my father's house. He owns his own house. He's been in Canada since 1920. And then I got arrested. It all happened so fast.

CALO: Romano, I spoke to some of the men here, and quite a few of them play music. Who knows how long we'll be here? Why don't you ask the commander for some instruments. It'll help with the morale. Ask him for some guitars, and throw in some mandolins.

ROMANO: That's good. We'll keep ourselves busy. I'm going to ask for books; I'm going to study the law. There's a court house in Pembroke. A judge will hear your request for release.

CALO: Talk to Paolo Maldini in Barracks No. 4, he's a professor. He'll help you. (*VITO starts coughing violently*) You need some medicine. We have rights. If not, they may as well kill us.

LUCA: That's what your people would do.

CALO: If what Mussolini is doing is so bad, explain what these people are doing to us?

LUCA: Name me one fucking thing that man has done that was good?

CALO: He made the trains run on time.

LUCA: The trains! The trains! Ha! That's all we've been hearing for the past ten years, Mussolini has made the trains run on time! I don't know about you, but we never had a problem with the trains. And since when did the Italians complain if a train was a half hour late? Italians are never on time.

LUCERNE and DUNNISON enter.

DUNNISON: At attention men! Will Romano Dicenzo step forward please.

ROMANO does so.

LUCERNE: Do you understand the instructions?

DUNNISON: (*pause*) Answer the Colonel when he addresses you!

ROMANO: Yes sir.

LUCA begins to walk away.

DUNNISON: At attention! (*LUCA stops*) The Colonel is talking. (*LUCA stares him down*)

LUCERNE: What's your name? (*pause, stares LUCA down*) What is your name?

LUCA: Fuck you!

LUCERNE: Too bad Mussolini doesn't have a man like you fighting for him.

LUCA: I'm not a Fascist. I'm not supposed to be here.

LUCERNE: Is anyone?

LUCA: There's been a mistake. This side of the camp is full of Italians. I'm not Italian.

LUCERNE: You're not?

LUCA: I'm Sicilian. My name is Luca Delferro. I don't belong here.

LUCERNE: Ah, I see. You're still angry at Garibaldi are you?

LUCA: Italy has never done anything for us.

LUCERNE: Perhaps you're right. But until your island gains its independence, you are regarded an Italian, and therefore an enemy of the state. Is that understood? We've gone quite a distance to make you feel right at home. Who's your Barracks Leader?

DUNNISON: Prisoner 432 was elected leader, sir.

LUCERNE: Which one is he?

DUNNISON: That would be Romano Dicenzo, sir.

LUCERNE: Well, then, this seems to be your lucky day. Are there any questions?

VITO coughs violently. ROMANO goes to his aid.

DUNNISON: In line, 432!

ROMANO: He needs help.

DUNNISON: I said in line!

ROMANO: (*he gets back in line*) Permission to speak, sir.

LUCERNE: Yes.

ROMANO: This man needs a doctor, sir. His cough doesn't sound good.

LUCERNE: I know the ploys of getting out of work details, my man, it will not work with me.

ROMANO: I think he's really sick, sir.

LUCERNE: Very well then. Captain Leblanc is the Camp Doctor. Should he find nothing wrong with him I will hold you with obstruction of Camp regulations, understood?

ROMANO: I can vouch for his sickness, sir.

LUCERNE: You better pray that he is sick. Sergeant, make sure he gets to the doctor.

DUNNISON: Yes sir.

VITO's coughing has subsided.

VITO: I don't need a doctor.

ROMANO: Yes you do.

LUCERNE: Mr. Dicenzo, you speak when you are spoken to in my presence.

ROMANO: Yes sir. But as Camp Spokesman, I just wanted....

LUCERNE: PERMISSION TO SPEAK, DO YOU UNDERSTAND!

ROMANO: (*pause, quietly*) Permission to speak, sir.

LUCERNE: Go ahead.

ROMANO: Yes well…this man here has been hit by one of the guards. We've been here for only a few hours, and already men are complaining about physical abuse.

LUCERNE: This is a war camp.

ROMANO: Yes sir, I understand that, but I have to say that I would rather be treated…what I mean to say, sir, is treat us as prisoners of war, sir, and not as guests. And as such, you will have to abide by the rules of the Geneva Convention. You may want to inform your guards that they are breaking the rules when they physically harm us. It's only a matter of time that the international press will know of this camp. Sir.

LUCERNE: Noted. I will remind you, Dicenzo, that as Camp Spokesman, I will hold you personally responsible for any breach of regulations. I will consider you and the entire population of the camp guilty. You have a job to do. Do it.

ROMANO: I will. Sir?

LUCERNE: Speak.

ROMANO: Since we don't know how long we'll be here…. I'm thinking of the camp morale. There are men here who can play music. We request some guitars and mandolins.

LUCERNE: Mandolins?

ROMANO: Our work detail will consist of cutting down trees, and repairing the bridge. We Italians work better knowing we have music to come home to.

LUCERNE: Is this a threat?

ROMANO: It's a fact, sir.

LUCERNE: Yes, well, I don't see any harm in music. You'll have your instruments if the men will play Vivaldi's Concerto for Mandolins.

CALO: Minghia! (*LUCERNE looks at CALO*) No problem. Uh…sir.

LUCERNE: I want to hear it by the end of the month or the instruments will be taken away. So you'll have your orchestra, I'll have my order. Back in line.

ROMANO: Thank you very much, Colonel. Thank you, sir. (*steps back in line*)

LUCERNE: And Sergeant, have the MP escort Mr. Delferro to solitary confinement. One week.

LUCERNE exits as DUNNISON salutes him.

DUNNISON: (*crosses over to the men*) You heard the Colonel. If you comply with the regulations, we'll get this done right.

VITO: What have we done? Why are we here?

DUNNISON: Our government feels that you men are dangerous to the country.

ROMANO: But we haven't been charged with anything.

VITO: I was born here.

DUNNISON: You've been arrested because you've done something wrong. That wrong will be dealt with by the government. The rest is up to the command to decide. Alright, men. You've heard the routine. In case you need to be reminded—see that tower over there? There will be guards there 24 hours a day. They've been able to hit jack rabbits from at least 500 yards. Don't try anything. I promise you will die. (*crosses to VITO*) You come with me. (*pause, turns to the men*) You haven't been charged?

ROMANO: No.

DUNNISON: Isn't that something? (*exits with VITO*)

CALO: (*pause*) How the fuck are we going to play Vivaldi? These men play tarantellas and love songs.

ROMANO: (*staring at LUCA*) What are you trying to do? Get us killed?

LUCA: Why don't you wake up? These stupid Canadians won't shoot anyone.

ROMANO: You don't know that. You probably have some family you want to get back to. Think of them.

LUCA: You have no idea who you're dealing with here. You just stay out of my way and there will be no problem. If you don't, you pay with your life.

DUNNISON: (*entering*) Delferro!

LUCA crosses to DUNNISON and they exit.

CALO: I can never figure out those Sicilians. He's as scared as the rest of us. You scared?

ROMANO: I'm scared for my wife.

Scene 2

The Camp Office, later that day. DUNNISON is looking over some papers at his desk. LUCERNE enters, as DUNNISON rises to attention.

LUCERNE: At ease, Sergeant. (*DUNNISON rubs his eyes*) Tired?

DUNNISON: No sir. Just need to rest my eyes, Colonel. I want to finish these letters tonight.

LUCERNE: Found anything?

DUNNISON: Nothing suspicious. Most of these are German.

LUCERNE: Transfer them to British Columbia. They'll take care of the Germans over there.

DUNNISON: A few of these letters were written by the Finnish prisoners. I didn't count on there being any Finnish prisoners, and so I don't have...I'm a little rusty with the language, you see, and I don't have a Finnish dictionary. I put in an order a week ago.

LUCERNE: You realize the Finns are great friends of the Germans?

DUNNISON: I'm aware of that, sir.

LUCERNE: I need to know everything that goes on here.

DUNNISON: I understand.

LUCERNE: Ignorance is not tolerated here, Sergeant. Our brothers and sisters are being killed over in Europe. I run a taut ship here, Dunnison. One more oversight like that, and you will be transferred. Understood? You will get your Finnish dictionary.

DUNNISON: That's all I need, sir.

LUCERNE: (*pause*) What do we have on Luca The Sicilian?

DUNNISON: According to his file, it's all underground activity. He's in close with Rocco Perri, who runs the rackets out of Hamilton. Perri controls everything from Windsor to Montréal including some parts of the United States.

LUCERNE: I had no idea we were harbouring gangsters in this camp.

DUNNISON: If history tells us the truth, these gangsters will form their gangs in the camps.

LUCERNE: I know. What do we have on Dicenzo?

DUNNISON: Nothing really. Ran a successful construction company in Montréal. Was at the forefront in the business. Nothing but steady growth since he moved to Canada.

LUCERNE: I don't trust him. It's always the less obvious you watch out for. By the time I'm through with him, I want him on his knees.

DUNNISON: Sir?

LUCERNE: The less obvious, Dunnison, remember that, the less obvious.

DUNNISON: Yes sir.

LUCERNE: Carry on.

DUNNISON: Got the order, sir, for guitars, mandolins and a couple of harmonicas. Just needs your signature.

LUCERNE: (*signs the form*) Do you like Vivaldi?

DUNNISON: Yes. But I listen to Bach.

LUCERNE: Carry on.

> *As the lights fade we hear ROMANO's letter over the sound system.*

ROMANO'S VOICE: My dearest, Maria. You don't know how much I miss you. My love for you feeds my very existence. My wish is that this letter finds you in good spirits. Do not worry about me. I'm well taken care of here. The army allows the prisoners to play their music. I spend my time reading books. Don't bother sending me anything but your kind words and your loving thoughts. Keep the food for yourself. Maybe you can send me my woolen sweater. It gets a little cool here at night. Maria, I have blown a kiss into the wind, tomorrow when you walk out and feel the early morning breeze upon your cheeks, it will be my kiss that touches you. Sleep well. I love you. Always. Romano.

Scene 3

MARIA appears waiting anxiously at a street corner M. LEFEBVRE, a lawyer, enters.

MARIA: Monsieur Lefebvre? (*pause*) I don't know if you remember me. My name is Maria Dicenzo. Romano's wife.

LEFEBVRE: (*Pause, he looks around*) Yes.

MARIA: Nobody knows I'm here.

LEFEBVRE: Look, I'm a really busy man…. I have people to see.

MARIA: If you just give me a minute, my husband has been taken away, it's been three months, I have no idea where he is. Just tell me, you of all people should know. Is he alive?

LEFEBVRE: You mean you don't know? (*pause*) They just announced it today. The prisoners are being held at a war camp in Petawawa. He's alive.

MARIA: Oh, God. Oh…sweet Jesus.

LEFEBVRE: I really have to go….

MARIA: Monsieur Lefebvre, I didn't want to compromise your position by coming into your office. But as my husband's lawyer, you can give me a minute.

LEFEBVRE: If my clients see me talking to you, I could lose everything. I'm a lawyer, my whole profession relies on credibility. Now what are you here for?

MARIA: I need your help.

LEFEBVRE: There's nothing I can do.

MARIA: You took my husband's money when it was good for you, why can't you just point me in the right direction?

LEFEBVRE: What do you want?

MARIA: My husband is innocent. Can't you get him released?

LEFEBVRE: Do you know what you're asking me to do? The Italians have been classified as Enemy Aliens. Now I have very important clients. What will they think of me if I help you?

MARIA: Do you think I'm your enemy?

LEFEBVRE: It doesn't matter what I think, it's what they think. I have a business to run.

MARIA: What about the pursuit of justice and upholding the law of the land?

LEFEBVRE: (*pause*) Do you know who accused your husband?

MARIA: No.

LEFEBVRE: You don't?

MARIA: I don't know anything. They just took him away. Do you see how wrong all of this is?

She suddenly gets a sharp pain in the abdomen.

LEFEBVRE: What's wrong?

MARIA: You know the company's been shut down, they seized everything.

LEFEBVRE: I'm aware of that.

MARIA: What about the land deal in Ville LaSalle? What happened to the money?

LEFEBVRE: It's all frozen.

MARIA: What about your commission?

LEFEBVRE: Look, I'll give you the money back, if that's what you want.

MARIA: No. You can have the money, I'm not going to interfere in my husband's business affairs. I just want you to help me.

LEFEBVRE: The most I can do...what I'll do is, I'll put some feelers out there amongst my colleagues. I'll see where they stand on this issue. If the coast is clear, I'll guide you to the proper authorities. My guess is that you would have to write a letter claiming Romano's innocence. We get the letter to a judge, and let the proper procedures take their due course. But this only works if there aren't any implications of corroboration on my part. I took care of Romano's legal work pertaining to his construction business, this is a whole different matter. And don't meet me here again. If we need to talk, I'll send you a message where you can meet me. Good luck. (*exits*)

> *MARIA gathers herself together and begins to leave. CENZO enters.*

MARIA: What are you doing here? Are you following me?

CENZO: Let's get out of the light. What did the lawyer say?

MARIA: Cenzo, I'm going to handle this through the law. Now leave me alone.

CENZO: I have something for you. (*he gives her an envelope*) I have to go now. (*we hear a police whistle in the distance*) Good luck! (*he runs off*)

> *A Policeman shouts: "You there! Stay right there!" More whistling. More shouting: "Come back here! Come back here! Jimmy, he ran that way, an Italian for sure, I tell'ya!" MARIA unwraps the parcel. She takes out some money. She looks off towards CENZO. As the lights fade we hear MARIA's letter over the sound system.*

MARIA'S VOICE: My dear Romano. My loyal and loving husband. I'm close to the end of my pregnancy, and with every passing day, I can feel the life growing inside me, the life that comes from your love, your strength, and your heart. Don't worry about me. I'm well taken care of by Teresina. Though she is an old lady, she has the strength of three women. Remember the sound of the crickets when we'd watch the sun go down? I hear them as I write to you. I hear them, and I can feel you. I am sending your sweater, winter is approaching. I await some news, a word, a whisper. I await your freedom. Think of a name for the child. Your loving wife, Maria.

Scene 4

> *Four months later. The barracks hut. CALO is strumming the mandolin. LUCA and VITO are playing cards. ROMANO enters carrying some papers.*

ROMANO: They're almost ready, guys. That mess hall's been set up for a symphony, make us proud tonight. (*distributes the letters*) Here's your mail. It's all been censored.

CALO: My hands are swollen from the work. How many trees do they want us to cut?

ROMANO: We need enough to last us the winter. How do you expect to feed that furnace?

VITO: All I do is paint all day. I need to come out and work with you guys. I can paint these barracks over and over, it doesn't change a thing. It's still a barracks.

ROMANO: I'll see what I can do. (*about the letters*) Anything good?

VITO: My father says the wine is good this year. He makes his own wine.

ROMANO: I'd love to have a sip of that. Hey, Vito, a nice plate of sausages, peppers, cheese, a smooth glass of red wine, it's heaven.

VITO: Stop it, you're making me horny.

ROMANO: Minghia, Vito, what the hell are you thinking about when I talk?

CALO: Look at this: "The weather is good." I swear, when I get out of here, I'm gonna teach my sister a lesson. What is she thinking? Who cares about the fucking weather? If I wanted a weather report, I could get it from Dunnison.

ROMANO: Alright, guys, I have the forms here. The judge in Pembroke will hear your case. Just tell the judge the truth. They seem to know everything. You have to sign over here, Calo. You should get your hearing within the month. Luca, yours is all in order. Now all the judge can do is recommend you for release, it's the Minister of Justice that makes the decision. Vito, you haven't filled out your form here. Don't you want to get out of here?

VITO: I don't want to face a judge, I didn't do anything.

CALO: That's what you're there for. You tell the judge you're innocent. What are you afraid of? It's a half hour drive to Pembroke. Just the drive is worth it.

ROMANO: Vito, if you want, I can ask to come with you. I don't think they'd mind.

VITO: No.

ROMANO: It's really no big deal, I'll tell them....

VITO: I said NO! I don't want to do it, now leave me alone with that!

CALO: Hey, Vito, come on, he's just trying to help. If there's something you don't want to tell us, fine. This is between you and the judge, nobody has to know a thing.

ROMANO: (*he reads one of the papers*) We have a complaint here.

CALO: What's wrong?

ROMANO: The mandolin orchestra. Some men are protesting the participation of Fascist musicians.

CALO: Who filed the complaint?

LUCA: I did.

CALO: You can't stop us from playing. You know how many hours we've put in rehearsing? The camp needs to hear some music.

LUCA: Not if it's played by Fascists.

CALO: Music is music. Can you believe this guy? What difference does it make if I play Vivaldi or someone else does? Romano, this can't go on.

LUCA: He's our camp spokesman. I filed a complaint, and I'm backed up by about eighty other men. It's your duty to see that we get our voices heard.

CALO: We're playing whether you like it or not.

ROMANO: Wait a minute, Calo. I have to abide by the rules.

CALO: You agree with this guy?

ROMANO: I'm saying, I have to bring it to the attention of the commander.

VITO: But if a mandolin is played by a Fascist, does it sound different?

CALO: A musical note is a musical note. I'd like to file a counter protest.

ROMANO: There's no such thing.

CALO: What do you mean there's no such thing? I protest his protest.

LUCA: I'll just protest your right to protest.

VITO: Oouw, ma vulite i a fanculo! You're making me dizzy with these protests!

ROMANO: Tomorrow we discuss this in the open and put it to a vote.

CALO: We have a concerto to play tonight. The Colonel is waiting.

LUCA: You'll have to cancel it.

CALO: You can't let him do this! Music is all I have in this camp! You can't take my music away from me!

ROMANO: It's not my decision.

CALO: Will you stop sitting on the fence, and take a position. What's the matter with you? You know who this guy is. You can't let him have his way. This is unbelievable! Music is music. This has nothing to do with Fascism!

LUCA: It does if you play it. It's called musical interpretation. What do you think, I'm a fucking idiot? It has everything to do with Fascism. Music is one of the ways Mussolini plays to your pride. We're in here because of him. You're so proud of your motherland. Are you so fucking blind? You saw those few weeks with the Germans. They got visits from the Swiss Consul General. On behalf of Berlin, the Germans got food, clothes, and money, to help them with their difficulties here. And us, what did we get? (*picks up a box of pencils*) Pencils. Fucking pencils! The Italian Embassy sends us pencils. How do we survive on that?

CALO: Spoken like a true wiseguy.

LUCA: (*puts a dagger to his throat*) You son of a bitch!

VITO: (*approaches LUCA*) Put it down, Luca. Luca, put it down.

LUCA puts down the dagger and conceals it.

ROMANO: Listen to me, both of you. Tomorrow I'm asking the commander that one of you be transferred to another barracks. I just can't have a Fascist and—you in the same room.

DUNNISON enters, followed by LUCERNE carrying a small box and a file.

DUNNISON: At attention men! (*the Italian men rise to attention*)

LUCERNE: (*entering*) As you were, gentlemen. Dunnison?

DUNNISON: We'll proceed in an orderly fashion. We start with Barracks No. 1 to No. 2 and so on. On my call you will proceed to the mess hall, take your seat, and enjoy the show.

LUCERNE: (*to CALO*) Why aren't you with the orchestra?

CALO: I was on my way.

ROMANO: We have a problem here. (*hands him the letter of protest*)

LUCERNE: (*reads*) I see. Eighty men are not the majority in this camp.

LUCA: If you give me another day, I can get that to three hundred.

LUCERNE: Don't you want music?

LUCA: Music, yes. Under the Fascists, it's propaganda.

LUCERNE: Romano, did you discuss this with the other hut leaders?

ROMANO: I just learned of it.

LUCERNE: Alright then. (*turns to VITO*) What do you think of all this?

VITO: Me, I'm hungry.

LUCERNE: How many Fascists in the Mandolin Orchestra?

CALO: A few of us. Does it make a difference? You promised us an orchestra.

LUCA: Listening to music played by Fascists is an insult to these men. We're all in here because of what he believes in. Your army is fighting his people as we speak.

CALO: Take my mandolin. I've been insulted enough. Do what you want.

LUCERNE: Aren't you the orchestra leader?

CALO: Yes I am.

DUNNISON: Sir, if I may? Let the men decide tonight. Let them play. If the men like what they hear, they'll let them know. If not, they'll hear about it. We have the camp waiting, sir.

LUCERNE: Alright, Calabrese, you'll have six hundred critics tonight, it's all in your hands.

DUNNISON: You received a package today, courtesy of the Italian Embassy. (*takes out a box of pencils from the box*) More pencils. I guess they expect you to do a lot of writing.

LUCERNE: Romano. Tomorrow I have a new work detail. We need a road built. I want you to supervise the work. Can you assemble the men you need tomorrow morning?

ROMANO: Yes sir.

LUCERNE: Dicenzo. We'll be in the open air tomorrow. You will remind your men that there is nowhere to run. The guards will shoot a warning first. If not obeyed, they will shoot to kill. Is that understood? Now. I want to hear some music. What's on the program tonight?

CALO: Vivaldi. As you requested.

LUCERNE: Well, let's hear it.

CALO: Just remember that we Calabrese outnumber you. You'll never have a majority here. Viva Italia! (*exits*)

VITO: Romano, put me on that road work tomorrow. Please.

ROMANO: You sure? (*VITO nods*) Alright then.

VITO: Thanks. You guys coming? I hope Calo makes us proud tonight. (*exits*)

LUCA looks at ROMANO and exits.

LUCERNE: Romano, stay. (*pause*) I see here that you have your appointment set in front of the judge.

ROMANO: Yes. Everything will be straightened out, I'm sure of it.

LUCERNE: What are your feelings towards Benito Mussolini?

ROMANO: What's this about?

LUCERNE: Answer the question.

ROMANO: I don't care for his politics.

LUCERNE: Do you feel that Mussolini's views are dangerous to the well being of this country?

ROMANO: Yes I do.

LUCERNE: Dunnison? (*he hands him the file*) I have here a list dated May 10, 1940. This is a list of names compiled by the RCMP in Montréal. It is a list of known and suspected Fascists. Your name is on this list. Do you care to explain this?

ROMANO: Sir, this can't be…. I never…. (*he advances towards LUCERNE, DUNNISON intervenes*) I'm sorry. It's a mistake. Will the judge see this list? Please, sir, I beg you. I am not a member of the Fascist Party. You have to believe me.

LUCERNE: This list here, says you are. My advice to you is to go to court better prepared to answer questions. You will have to explain your name here.

ROMANO: Sir….

LUCERNE: Don't you ever lie to me again. Is that clear?

ROMANO: But sir….

DUNNISON: Let it go, Romano. Just take it easy.

Vivaldi's "Concerto For Mandolins" plays in the background. ROMANO listens as we hear ROMANO's letter over the sound system.

ROMANO'S VOICE: Maria, beyond the barbed wire fence is some of the most beautiful land you'll ever set eyes upon. As I gaze over and beyond the hills, I'm reminded of how enormous this country is. I've made some friends in the camp. I'm proud of our people; we have doctors, professors, shoe makers, musicians, so many talented people. Tell Lorenzo that his son is fine. He's a brave young man. He eats a lot. Maria, I see hope beyond the barbed wire fence. And I see you.

Scene 5

MARIA appears writing a letter, CENZO stands about. Later that night.

CENZO: ...you know that the letters are read....

MARIA: I know.

CENZO: Maria, make it real...you know...like with the love thing....

MARIA: What love thing?

CENZO: I don't mean any disrespect, but make love to him in the letter...the military guy who reads it...it's going to drive him nuts.

MARIA: Cenzo....

CENZO: Trust me...just be nice about it: Ti amo, je t'aime, I love you...my fingers touch your...parrabee-parraba.... I caress your...parraboom.... I lie on top of your body as our lips touch each others' souls...my breasts...well...you know...that's your thing....

MARIA: Cenzo, what the hell are you thinking?

CENZO: Trust me, write it....

LEFEBVRE enters.

LEFEBVRE: Mrs. Dicenzo. I'm sorry, I didn't mean to startle you. Cenzo. How are you? (*pause*) I won't be long. (*pause*) Maria. Since we last spoke, I made some inquiries into your husband's case. Now please understand, that my study of law is corporate, not criminal.

MARIA: You can't help me?

LEFEBVRE: No. Listen. You see, that is what intrigued me. The Petawawa arrests fall under the jurisdiction of criminal law, not corporate. I spoke to a colleague of mine, who shall remain nameless...a Crown Prosecutor...he told me absolutely nothing I didn't already know. But he led me to a judge. At no time in this country's history, have such sweeping arrests taken place based on one's ethnic origin. Never. One can understand the government's concerns—it's when you start to take the whole picture apart, and begin to examine the brush strokes, where you see the smaller details.

MARIA: Such as? (*she has a contraction*)

LEFEBVRE: (*pause*) As I pursued the obvious, it led me nowhere. I looked straight into my own world. The world of money. That means business. Big business. Part of the Petawawa arrests were aimed at destroying Italian business interests. (*shows her a file*) You see this? This is the land deal I closed for Romano. You see here? This has been approved by the city. This land deal is totally above board. You see that signature there? This man was a city official. (*pause*) Now, as Romano's lawyer, I contested the confiscation of his land. I obtained a copy...as was

78

my right...from the Custodian Of Alien Property....
(*shows her a file*) See here. This document is what
took the land away from your husband. Now. Look
at that signature there. (*MARIA does so*) It's the
same man who first approved of the deal.

MARIA: Monsieur Lefebvre, please, what are you telling
me here?

LEFEBVRE: Don't you see? This was all planned. This
signature here...this Mr. MacDonald, is one of the
most influential city officials.

MARIA: If all he wanted was that land, why didn't he
just purchase it himself?

LEFEBVRE: Because Romano would've bought other
land, and built there. The goal was to destroy him.
Now, Maria, listen. What I'm telling you here is
what's going on at the top. They are untouchable.
So long as the directive of the government is in
place, they are protected by the law of the land. See
this paper here? This destroyed Dicenzo
Construction. But they needed someone to do their
dirty work.

MARIA: Informers?

LEFEBVRE: Yes. And who better than rival businessmen. Who better than fellow Italians? They were
provided with a means with which to get rid of their
competitors. Now this is all I can tell you. I've given
you the picture from the top. What I don't know is
what's at the bottom. My advice to you is to stay out
of it. It's too dangerous.

MARIA: My husband is in a prison camp.

LEFEBVRE: We'll have to use the system. We have no
other way. (*gives her another file*) This is a letter from
me, attesting to Romano's character. Send it to him
in Petawawa. He'll have his day in front of a judge.

CENZO: I want to know who the informer is.

LEFEBVRE: It's someone close. Very close. We'll never know. Just let it go.

MARIA: I take it you'll be helping me.

LEFEBVRE: We're not all sharks, you know. Romano was good to me.

CENZO: Sending my brother a letter stating he's a good guy isn't enough.

MARIA: Cenzo, stay out of this. We're taking care of it.

CENZO: Who's the middle guy? Who are the authorities using to destroy us?

LEFEBVRE: I don't have that information. I really have to go....

CENZO: You can start off by speaking to the arresting officer.

LEFEBVRE: That will get you nowhere.

CENZO: What are they going to do with that land?

LEFEBVRE: It's going to be auctioned off.

CENZO: That not only kills Dicenzo Construction, it buries us for good.

LEFEBVRE: It's the law. The Custodian Of Alien Property has been set up to do exactly that.

CENZO: You just be there at the auction to find out who buys the land. And you'll find your informer.

LEFEBVRE: I don't think so, Mr. Dicenzo.

CENZO: I'll do it myself.

BRUNO: (*entering*) Maria, are you okay?

MARIA: Monsieur Lefebvre, this is my cousin Bruno Benevento. This is Romano's lawyer.

LEFEBVRE: Pleasure. Have we met?

BRUNO: No. Romano kept me out of the business end of things. What brings you here this time of night?

MARIA: Monsieur Lefebvre is helping me get Romano released.

BRUNO: Are you still handling his business affairs?

LEFEBVRE: As you know, there's not much to do. I really shouldn't be talking about this.

BRUNO: (*MARIA has a contraction*) What's wrong? (*pause*) We should get you to a hospital.

MARIA: I'm not due for another couple of weeks.

LEFEBVRE: Do you have a doctor?

CENZO: Why?

LEFEBVRE: Some hospitals refuse to treat Italians. They consider you undesirable.

BRUNO: This is ridiculous, she's pregnant!

LEFEBVRE: They arrested some women too, for your information. (*pause*) If there's nothing else, I'll be going now.

LORENZO enters.

LORENZO: Buona sera a tutti. Senti, Cenzo, i sordi chi ci detti a vostru fratti pe a casa, me l'hanno fregatti. Capisci? Mi scusate, Maria, ma stu sbagliu l'amu aggiustare.
[Good evening to all. Listen, Cenzo, the money I gave to your brother for the house, they stole it. Understand? Excuse me, Maria, but this error must be corrected.]

CENZO: Did you hear that? What happened to his money...the down payment on the house we were supposed to build in Ville LaSalle?

LEFEBVRE: It's all frozen....

LORENZO: Chi chistu?
[Who is this?]

CENZO: L'avocato di Romano.
[Romano's lawyer.]

LORENZO: Ahh. Alora me potisse aiutari.
[Ahh. So then you can help me.]

LEFEBVRE: What's he saying?

CENZO: He wants his money back.

LEFEBVRE: That's impossible.

LORENZO: Impossibile? Stu cazzo! Ma guarda cha stu mucousu, non mi dire che e impossibile che ti rumpu la faccia!
[Impossible? My ass! Look at this snot-face, don't tell me that it's impossible because I'll break your face!]

MARIA: Lorenzo, calmati!
[Lorenzo, calm down!]

LEFEBVRE: Tell him that it's the law.

LORENZO: U law? Ti tengu io u law! Che sistema di leggi ndavite cha, quando u guviernu ti freggano i soldi?
[The law? I'll give you the law! What kind of system is this when the government steals your money?]

BRUNO: Lorenzo, per piacere….
[Lorenzo, please.]

LORENZO: IO VOGLIO I SOLDI MIEI! E BASTA!
[I WANT MY MONEY BACK! AND THAT'S THAT!]

CENZO: I understand shutting down Italian businessmen. But this guy is just a grocer. He put his life savings into a home that Romano was going to build for him.

LEFEBVRE: These laws affect the entire Italian population!

LORENZO: Cenzo, di a stu pezzo novanta, che due uomini sunu venuti per avertirmi. Mi hanno detto che se mi compro na casa di Romano, le cose vanno male.
[Cenzo, tell this silly big shot that two men have warned me. They told me that if I buy one of Romano's houses, things will go very bad for me.]

CENZO: He's already been threatened by two men, if he continues to do business with Dicenzo Construction.

LEFEBVRE: Who threatened him?

LORENZO: Uno era italiano che si chiamava Peppino. Quel altro parlava inglese....
[One was Italian, his name was Peppino. The other guy spoke English.]

HÉLÈNE enters.

HÉLÈNE: What is all that shouting? People are scared you know.

MARIA: Everybody, let's just go inside....

LORENZO: Ascortami. Ci sta qualcuno nel nostro quartiere che sta parlando alla polizia. Un traditore! Stat'attento. Non ci puo mai sapere.
[Listen to me all of you. There is someone in the neighbourhood who is talking to the police. A traitor! You never know.]

A POLICEMAN enters.

POLICEMAN: Everybody stay calm. We could do this very quietly. I'm looking for a man named Cenzo Dicenzo. I have here a warrant for his arrest.

LEFEBVRE: Let me see. (*he hands him the arrest warrant*)

POLICEMAN: (*to HÉLÈNE*) Hélène, qu-est ce que tu fais ici?
[Hélène, what are you doing here?]

HÉLÈNE: C'est la propriétié de mon père. J'ai le droit d'être ici.
[This is my father's property. I have the right to be here.]

POLICEMAN: I assume you are Mr. Dicenzo. (*pause*) Let me see some identification.

LORENZO: Che sta dicendo?
[What's he saying?]

LEFEBVRE: Cenzo wait, put your wallet away. Où est votre partenaire?
[Where's your partner?]

POLICEMAN: Quel partenaire?
[What partner?]

LEFEBVRE: Je suis avocat. Vous ne faites pas d'arrestations tout seul. Vous me prenez pour un idiot? Où est votre partenaire?
[I'm a lawyer. You can't make an arrest alone. Do you think I'm an idiot? Where's your partner?]

HÉLÈNE: Es-tu venu pour le tuer?
[Have you come to kill him?]

POLICEMAN: Absolument pas.
[Absolutely not.]

LEFEBVRE: Donc où est votre partenaire?
[So, where is your partner?]

POLICEMAN: C'est une affaire de police….
[This is a police matter….]

LEFEBVRE: Je vais tout de suite aller voir votre capitaine. S'il me dit que vous avez fait quelque chose d'irrégulier, vous allez perdre votre badge. Compris?
[I'm going to see your captain right now. If he tells me that you've done anything fishy, you're going to lose your badge. Understood?]

HÉLÈNE: Qui est ton indicateur?

[Who's your informant?]

POLICEMAN: Je ne peux pas te le dire.

[I can't say.]

HÉLÈNE: Alors, on peut pas t'aider. Sors de ma propriété. Tout de suite.

[So, we can't help you. Off my property. Now.]

POLICEMAN: Hé, toi, tu ne peux pas me parler de même.

[Hey, you can't talk to me like that.]

LORENZO: Ma che cazzo vo chistu? Hey Missyou, c'est homme içi, very very good man. I speak for him. C'é lo faccio vedere io stu rimbambito!

[What the fuck does he want? Hey, mister, this man here is a very very good man. I speak for him. I'll show this idiot!]

LEFEBVRE: Lorenzo, s'il vous plâit.

[Lorenzo, please.]

LORENZO: (*to CENZO*) Ma hai fatto qualcosa? (*CENZO shakes his head*) E allora? Che te ne frega?

[Have you done something wrong? So then? What the fuck do you care?]

POLICEMAN: You're going to have to come with me.

HÉLÈNE: Tu touches à un cheveu de cet homme, tu ne verras jamais plus l'intérieur d'un poste de police. Compris?

[If you touch one hair on this man, you'll never see the inside of a police station again. Understood?]

POLICEMAN: Es-ce qu'il y a quelque chose entre vous deux?

[Is there something going on between you two?]

LEFEBVRE: Elle n'est pas obligée de répondre à vos questions.

[She doesn't have to answer your questions.]

MARIA: (*she has a contraction*) Oh, my God....

LORENZO: Chi succede?
[What happened?]

BRUNO: Sta nascendo la creatura.
[She's giving birth.]

LORENZO: Ma sta crepandu. Hamma'iere al ospedale. Missyou, help us, she make baby.
[She's going to burst. We have to go to the hospital. Mister, help us, she make baby.]

CENZO: We have to get her to the hospital. She's going to have it now.

POLICEMAN: You stay right there, mister.

HÉLÈNE: Luc, c'est vraiment pas le moment.
[Luc, this really isn't a good time.]

LEFEBVRE: (*furious*) Regardez ce mandat! Ce n'est même pas signé par un juge. Qui vous a donné l'idée de faire ça?
[Look at this warrant! It's not even signed by a judge. Who told you to do this?]

POLICEMAN: Tu ne sais pas de quoi tu parles
[You don't know what you're talking about.]

HÉLÈNE: (*she looks at the arrest warrant*) Qui t'a donné l'idée de faire ça?
[Who told you to do this?]

POLICEMAN: Eh, Hélène, voyons-donc. Laisse moi tranquille.
[Come on, Hélène, leave me alone.]

HÉLÈNE: Tu gagnes beaucoup d'argent avec ces arrestations absurdes? Qui te paye? Dis-le moi. Veux-

tu que je parle à ta mère? Oui ou non? Qu'est-ce
qu'elle va penser d'un fils qui arrête les innocents?
[Do you make a lot of money off these ridiculous arrests? Who
pays you? Tell me. Do you want me to speak to your mother?
What will she think about having a son who arrests innocent
people?]

POLICEMAN: Mais voyons....
[Come on....]

MARIA: Wait a minute. I'm tired of all this.... I want to
know who accused this man here?

POLICEMAN: There's been no accusation, it's just a
precautionary....

MARIA: Who put you up to this?

POLICEMAN: I will remind you that you are the enemy
here. I have a job to do. Now this was a simple
mistake, let's just let it go.

MARIA: Who had my husband arrested? (*she has another
contraction*)

BRUNO: Oh, my God, this is bad.

LORENZO: Missyou, tu vas prendre ton auto, e
portiammo Maria al ospedale.... (*calling out*)
Teresina, sta nascendo il piccirillo!
[Mister, you go get your car, and we'll bring Maria to the
hospital.... Teresina, the little baby is coming out!]

POLICEMAN: What is this man saying?

CENZO: Can we use your car to bring this lady to the
hospital?

POLICEMAN: Well that's not police business.

LORENZO: Ma stu citrullo ancora qua sta! Missyou,
why you no help?
[This idiot is still here! Mister, why don't you help us?]

BRUNO: Look, officer, can't you rush this lady to the hospital?

POLICEMAN: No, but I'll provide you with an escort. Now get the lady in a car.

The men attempt to get MARIA up. But she is in too much pain.

CENZO: Okay, just take it easy now. Breathe.

LORENZO: Dio aiutacci! (*calling out*) Teresina! Sbrigati! Ma mia mugliera che cazzo sta facendu…. (*calling out*) Teresina!
[God help us! Teresina! Hurry! What the fuck is my wife doing…. Teresina!]

POLICEMAN: Moi là, j'ai jamais vu quelque chose comme ça. Jamais, tabernac! (*exits*)
[Boy, I've never seen anything like this. Never!]

LORENZO: Hey, Missyou, dove vai! Cretino!
[Hey, mister, where are you going! You cretin!]

LEFEBVRE: Will you tell this man to keep it down. Italians are still being arrested you know!

LORENZO: Ma va fanculo! Capisce, paesano! Tu, per chi lavoro? Guido Lombardo?
[Fuck you! Understand, paesano! Who do you work for? Guido Lombardo?]

LEFEBVRE: What did he say?

HÉLÈNE: Will you men stop arguing, and come help me!

LORENZO: (*overlapping*) You, Missyou, you work for Guido Lombardo? You people, you all the same… siete tutti pezzi novanta! Facite u big-a-shot, e mi parlate cussi…
[You, mister, you work for Guido Lombardo? You people, you are all the same…you're all a bunch of silly big shots! You play the big shot, and you speak to me like this.]

LEFEBVRE: You listen to me, Lorenzo, you should not mention that name here. Understand? Tell him he can get in very serious trouble for that.

CENZO: Lorenzo, zitto!
[Lorenzo, quiet!]

LORENZO: Perche? Lo trovu io stu Guido Lombardo, e fazzu io la giustizia! Madonna mia! Sta povera figlia! Hey, Missyou, you go talk to u cappu da pulizia! Maria she need Romano.
[Why? I'll find this Guido Lombardo, and I'll make some justice! My God! This poor girl! Hey, mister, you go talk to the head of the police! Maria needs Romano.]

LEFEBVRE: Will you tell this man to shut up!

LORENZO: Hey, shut-upa tu! Capisci! Cenzo, Bruno, aiutatemi.... Teresina! Teresina! Sta nascendo u piccirillu! (*the men succeed in getting MARIA up*)
[You shut up! Understand! Cenzo, Bruno, help me.... Teresina! Teresina! The little one is going to come out!]

MARIA: (*she keeps breathing heavily*) Oh my God!

LEFEBVRE: They may not admit her in the hospital!

BRUNO: I'm going to take her.

LEFEBVRE: No. Stay. I'll take her. (*crosses to MARIA*) They won't let any of you in.

LORENZO: Cha detto?
[What did he say?]

BRUNO: Non potemo andare, Lorenzo...
[We can't go, Lorenzo.]

LORENZO: Hey, Missyou, ma mo mi stai propio scassiare i palli!
[Hey, mister, now you're really starting to break my balls!]

LEFEBVRE: Okay, fine, I'll go with Lorenzo.... (*they hold up Maria as they begin to walk her out*)

LORENZO: (*to LEFEBVRE*) Hey, Missyou, facciamo chianu chianu...Maria...non ti preoccupare.... (*they exit*)
[Hey, mister, we'll go nice and slowly...nice and slowly.... Maria...don't worry.]

CENZO: Don't worry, Maria, you'll be fine.... (*long pause*) I should go with them.

HÉLÈNE: No, you heard what he said.

BRUNO: I'm going anyway.

CENZO: (*to BRUNO*) Hey, Bruno, wait a minute. Do you know who this guy is?

BRUNO: Who?

CENZO: Guido Lombardo.

BRUNO: No. Never heard of him. (*pause*) Why?

CENZO: This guy wants me arrested.

BRUNO: You don't know that.... I'll see you later.... (*exits*)

CENZO: Hélène, I'm going to be an uncle! (*he embraces her*)

HÉLÈNE: Cenzo. I don't like this. Something is going on here. Why are they after you?

CENZO: They took my brother, they want me too.

HÉLÈNE: What kind of life is this? I've waited so long for this, and I don't feel it's mine yet. How long will this go on? Look how much I've sacrificed for you, and I don't really know you. I want you, but I need to know you. No more secrets, I want everything....

CENZO: I need to get my brother out of the prison camp. My life is here now. With you. (*pause*) Look. Let's lay it all out tonight. Okay? No more secrets. In Italy we used to do this thing—with a glass of wine we share the truth. Because the wine is from the earth, and in its presence, one should not lie, because the wrath of time is in every drop. Our fathers taught us that wine is like the heavens, it sees everything. This comes down to us from the Caesars. (*they kiss*) Let's go inside Maria's.... (*playful*) I'm going to hide, you come find me.... (*exits*)

> *The lights fade on the scene, as MARIA's letter is heard over the sound system.*

MARIA'S VOICE: Romano, our baby is born. She is a beautiful little girl. She has your eyes, and already she smiles. Her name is Chiara. You are right. Our baby will be as a light who guides us through the good and the bad. Chiara: the clear and lighted one. I kiss her for you. I must feed her now.

Scene 6

> *The next day. M. BEAUCHAMP appears waiting. HÉLÈNE enters.*

M. BEAUCHAMP: Tiens, prends les clés et ouvres le magasin. J'arrive dans quelques minutes.
[Here, take the keys and open up the store. I'll be there in a few minutes.]

HÉLÈNE: Où allez-vous?
[Where are you going?]

M. BEAUCHAMP: Je vais voir Maria. J'ai l'avis d'expulsion.
[I'm going to see Maria. I have the eviction notice.]

HÉLÈNE: La situation est plus calme. Tout est correct.
[Things have calmed down now. We're okay.]

M. BEAUCHAMP: Ne t'en mêles pas. Je dois le faire. J'ai trouvé des nouveaux locataires.
[Stay out of this. What has to be done will be done. I found some new tenants.]

HÉLÈNE: Les Dicenzo n'ont rien fait du mal. Papa, réfléchissez. Vous réagissez trop violemment.
[The Dicenzos have done nothing wrong. Papa, think of what you're doing. You're overreacting.]

M. BEAUCHAMP: Ah, oui? Et qu'est-ce que qu'un policier faisait sur ma propriété hier soir? T'étais au courant? Qu'est-ce qu'il voulait? Les gens du quartier croient que je mijote quelque chose. Je ne supporte pas ça. J'ai mon commerce, bon Dieu!
[Am I? Why was there a policeman on my property last night? Did you know? What did he want? People in the neighbourhood think I may be up to something. I can't have that. I run a business for God's sake!]

HÉLÈNE: C'était un malentendu.
[It was a misunderstanding.]

M. BEAUCHAMP: Et il faut que je confronte mes clients aujourd'hui. Arrêtes de les excuser, veux-tu? De quel côté es-tu?
[And I have to face the customers in the store today. Will you stop defending them! Whose side are you on anyway?]

HÉLÈNE: Père Michel est au courant?
[Does Father Michel know about this?]

M. BEAUCHAMP: Ne joues pas ce jeu avec moi. Ça n'a rien à voir avec l'église. Père Michel lui-même doit obéir à la loi. Il va appuyer ma décision de renvoyer les Dicenzo parce que je protège ma famille.
[Don't you play that game with me. This is not the Church's business. Father Michel himself has to obey the law. He will support my decision to evict the Dicenzos because I'm protecting my family.]

HÉLÈNE: Ah, oui? Il vous appuyez?
[Really? Will he support your decision?]

M. BEAUCHAMP: Ben sûr. De toute façon, comment va-t-il savoir?
[Of course he will. Anyway, how will he know?]

HÉLÈNE: Quand Maria va aller faire baptiser son bébé!
[When Maria gets her baby baptized!]

M. BEAUCHAMP: Comment?
[What?]

HÉLÈNE: Avez vous oublié qu'elle était enceinte?
[Or did you forget that she was pregnant?]

M. BEAUCHAMP: Elle a accouché quand?
[When did she have the baby?]

HÉLÈNE: Hier soir. Vous allez expulser un bébé de sa maison. Vous pourriez dormir tranquille? Rendez-moi service: quand vous donnerez à Maria l'avis d'expulsion, expliquez-le au bébé.
[Last night. You'll be evicting a baby from a home. How can you have that on your conscience? Do me a favour. When you give Maria this eviction notice, I want you to explain it to the baby.]

M. BEAUCHAMP: Ça suffit!
[Enough!]

HÉLÈNE: Je vous verrai au marché.
[I'll see you at the store.]

M. BEAUCHAMP: Hélène. Tu connais les Italiens, ils ont la famille en masse pour s'entre-aider. Pourquoi tu t'impliques comme ça?
[Hélène. Listen to me, you know the Italians, they have plenty of family to help each other out. Why are you involving yourself like this?]

HÉLÈNE: Comme quoi, papa? Comme quoi? Comme une bonne chrétienne, comme vous m'avez élevée? Comme quoi?
[Like what, papa? Like what? Like the good Christian girl that you raised me to be? Like what?]

M. BEAUCHAMP: Ça n'a rien à voir.
[That has nothing to do with it.]

HÉLÈNE: Oui! Cela a tout à voir! Nous sommes tous mis à l'épreuve, et la seule solution pour vous: l'explusion d'une mère et son bébé. Vous n'avez pas honte?! (*pause*) De quoi avez vous peur? Maria a toujours payé son loyer. Les temps sont durs maintenant, qu'est-ce qui vous garantis que les nouveaux locataires pourront payer chaque mois?
[It has everything to do with it! Everything! We are all being tested here, and this is what you come up with? The eviction of a mother and her baby? Have you no shame? What are you really afraid of? Maria has always paid the rent. Times are hard now, what guarantee will you have that your new tenants can pay on time every month?]

M. BEAUCHAMP: (*pause, he rips up the eviction notice*) Bon. Je ne veux plus en parler.
[Fine. I won't argue with you.]

HÉLÈNE: Papa, c'est honorable.
[Papa, you're doing the right thing.]

M. BEAUCHAMP: Tu as pris la décision pour nous aujourd'hui; t'es mieux de prier que tu te feras pas blesser. (*exits*)
[You made the decision for us today; you just better pray you don't get hurt.]

HÉLÈNE: C'est promis, papa, promis.
[I won't, papa, I promise you I won't.]

Scene 7

LORENZO appears in the middle of the street.

LORENZO: (*to the neighbourhood*) GUIDO LOMBARDO! Se mi senti, ti sto aspettare! Tu si nu vigliaccu! Mi senti? Tu m'hai ruvinato la mia vita! E adesso devi pagare con il tuo sangue! GUIDO LOMBARDO! Tu sei proprio un diavolo! Perche non ti fai vedere? Ricordati, che la tua vita non vale tre soldi! You people who speaka eenglish.... Guido Lombardo is very very bad man! The mother of Lombardo is a dog! No listen to him. He tell lies of the Italians! He not our friend! Bastardo! (*He quiets down. He sees someone in the distance and exits.*)

[GUIDO LOMBARDO! If you hear me, I'm waiting for you! You are a coward! You hear me? You've ruined my life! And now you must pay with your blood! GUIDO LOMBARDO! You are the devil himself! Why don't you show yourself? Remember, your life is not worth three cents! You people who speak English.... Guido Lombardo is a very very bad man! The mother of Lombardo is a dog! Don't listen to him. He tell lies about the Italians! He is not our friend! Bastard!]

Scene 8

Later that night. MARIA is waiting at a street corner. Two men enter.

MAN 1: Watch my back.

MAN 2: You sure about this?

MAN 1: You got something better to do? (*pause*) Then shut your trap. (*he approaches MARIA*) Nice evening, eh, ma'am?

MARIA: Yes it is.

MAN 1: You been asking a lot of questions. Don't you know that right's been taken away from you?

MARIA: I'm waiting for my husband.

MAN 1: What the fuck do I care, who you're waiting for!

MARIA: I have nothing to do with you.

MAN 1: You fucking wop!

MAN 2: Hey, come on, man, you don't need to....

MAN 1: Shut up! You ever get fucked by Mussolini? I hear he fucks all the Italian women he wants.

MARIA: (*makes a run for it*) Please, help me!

> *MAN 2 stops her, as MAN 1 knocks MARIA to the ground.*

MAN 1: You fucking wop! (*kicks her viciously*) This is for learning you a lesson, which is don't ask no more questions about nobody. (*kicks her*) Got that?

> *CENZO appears suddenly with a piece of wood, knocks MAN 1 over the back and immobilizes him. MAN 2 runs off.*

CENZO: Maria, Maria. You okay? These fucking little bastards. Did they hurt you? Did they hurt you?

MARIA: No. I'm fine.

CENZO: You just wait here.

MARIA: Let's just go.

CENZO: NO! I've had enough. (*crosses to the MAN, takes out a knife*) Alright. You see this. I'm going to cut your fucking balls, and let you choke on them.

MARIA: Cenzo, they'll arrest you!

CENZO: NO! I don't care anymore.

MAN 1: Don't hurt me!

CENZO: (*puts the knife to his throat*) There's no one around. No one. I could kill you right now, and no one will know about it. Wouldn't that be something?

MAN 1: Please don't do it. Please. I'm just a kid.

CENZO: A kid! You call yourself a kid! (*CENZO moves to stab him*)

MARIA: NO! CENZO! Put the knife down! Put it down! (*CENZO freezes*) This won't solve anything.

CENZO: Give me one good reason why this man should live?

MARIA: Because I'm telling you.

CENZO: (*he takes out the MAN's wallet*) I have your name now. Who sent you here? Who sent you here? (*pause*) I'm giving you three seconds, and then there's going to be blood. One…two…three….

MAN 1: Guido Lombardo.

CENZO: Guido sent you here to kill her?

MAN 1: Just to rough her up. I was supposed to scare her!

CENZO: Why? (*pause*) Why?

MAN 1: I don't know. He just wants her to stop asking questions.

CENZO: (*spits on the MAN*) You see this knife? Remember it. I could've killed you tonight.

MAN 1: Let me go, please.

CENZO: You want your freedom?

MAN 1: Please.

CENZO: (*grabs him by the crotch*) I never forget a face, never. If I see your face again, I'll kill you and your whole fucking family. Got that? (*lets him go, MAN 1* *runs away*) Did you speak to anyone about Guido Lombardo?

MARIA: No. Did you?

CENZO: (*pause*) No...Yes, I...that night—

MARIA: Who did you tell?

CENZO: It's not important now. Alright, Maria. Now we do it my way.

MARIA: Let's go home.

CENZO: Are you okay?

MARIA: Yes.

CENZO: Maria....

MARIA: I'm fine....

CENZO: Maria....

MARIA: I'm fine...I'm fine.

CENZO is at MARIA's side as the lights fade slowly to black.

ACT THREE

Scene 1

*Pembroke, Ontario. The court house. A year later.
ROMANO stands in front of the JUDGE holding
some papers. The JUDGE's voice is heard over the
sound system.*

JUDGE: Mr. Dicenzo, Romano. Step forward, please.
What do you have to say?

ROMANO: Sir, if I may....

JUDGE: Please refer to the bench as My Lord.

ROMANO: My Lord, may I approach the bench?

JUDGE: Approach.

ROMANO: I have here some letters sent to me at
Petawawa from citizens of Canada. People who can
attest to my background. Here is a letter from a Mr.
Lefebvre, my lawyer. My Lord, I have here over
thirty letters, they come from all over Montréal,
Quebec, and some parts of Ontario. They can speak
of my honesty, and of my claim to innocence.
(*pause*) My Lord, if I may?

JUDGE: Go ahead.

ROMANO: I have been accused of being a Fascist. I do
not know who my accuser is. This accusation has
landed me in a prison camp. My business has been

destroyed. I have a wife and a child whom I have never met. My question to you, can I meet my accuser?

JUDGE: That information is confidential.

ROMANO: I understand. But can the state vouch for the veracity of the accuser?

JUDGE: The sources are said to be reliable.

ROMANO: Then what am I charged with?

JUDGE: You are being accused of being a Fascist, dangerous to the state.

ROMANO: Where is the proof?

JUDGE: Mr. Dicenzo, you have to understand that under the War Measures Act, the government has enacted the Defence Of Canada Regulations, which empowers the state to take such measures. Under the circumstances, you must concede some time for the authorities to verify the backgrounds of the accused. We are at war.

ROMANO: Then may I submit one more item.

JUDGE: You may.

ROMANO: This is a letter from the Quebec Minister of Labour. He will verify not only my record as an upstanding citizen, but as one whose devotion was only to his adopted country. Canada.

JUDGE: How are you connected to the Minister of Labour?

ROMANO: My plans are rather big, My Lord. I was going to build a city in Ville LaSalle. I needed the cooperation of the Minister.

JUDGE: Anything else?

ROMANO: You have my life in front of you. I can give nothing more. I ask only the respect accorded to a human being. My Lord, I have been reduced to nothing. I was once a proud man, I now have a record of being a prisoner of war, a record that stands on an accusation, with no proof. At the end of the day, it will be only the record that counts. How can I look my daughter in the face? How will I embrace her and ask for her trust?

JUDGE: Mr. Dicenzo. A courtroom is meant to look only at the facts. Emotion should never come to play in a decision concerning the rule of law. However, you have provided sufficient evidence to your credibility, the veracity of which can be corroborated. You understand that final permission for your release rests with the Ministry of Justice. This courtroom can only make its recommendations. (*pause*) How old is your child?

ROMANO: Two years old, My Lord.

JUDGE: Yes. Thank you.

Scene 2

The men appear in the barracks hut. Camp Petawawa. Early morning. CALO is strumming the mandolin. LUCA and VITO are playing cards. ROMANO enters.

CALO: Any word from the judge? (*ROMANO shakes his head*) You're out of here, let me tell you. Keeping you here is such an embarrassment to them. It defies any sense of their justice system. What are you going to do when you get out?

ROMANO: First thing, I have to get acquainted with my daughter. Then, I'm going to take my wife, hold on, and never let go.

VITO: Okay, stop now, I'm getting these thoughts.

CALO: Minghia, Vito, it doesn't take much to excite you does it?

VITO: That, and with the music playing, forget about it. I'm on a hill somewhere riding a horse with a woman behind me. Hey, Calo, 'Na Bella Napolitana.

CALO and VITO: (*singing*)
    'Na bella napolitana
    Cha vocca rossa, capelli neri, occhi bruni
    Caminava sola sola
    O sta bella napolitana
    [I saw a beautiful Neapolitan girl
    With her red mouth, black hair, brown eyes
    She was walking all alone
    Oh this beautiful Neapolitan girl]

    Ma gia spusa, ma gia spusa
    Cu sta bella femena
    Ma gia spusa, ma gia spusa
    Cu sta bella femena
    [I fell in love, I fell in love
    With this beautiful girl
    I fell in love, I fell in love
    With this beautiful girl]

    Ma giu mis a canta
    Pe' sta bella napolitana
    Ma guardatu pe nu mumentu
    E u core si mis a scuaglia
    [I started to sing
    For this beautiful Neapolitan girl
    She looked at me for a moment
    And my heart just started to melt]

Ma gia spusa, ma gia spusa
Cu sta bella femena
Ma gia spusa, ma gia spusa
E ma port o Canada.
[I fell in love, I fell in love
With this beautiful girl
I fell in love, I fell in love
And I'll bring her home to Canada.]

VITO: You sound just like my father when he sings.
Chu'la fisarmonica, e cantavamo tutto la iurnata.
[With the accordian, we'd sing all night long.]

DUNNISON enters the hut.

DUNNISON: Let's go men, mess hall. Lunch is served.

CALO: Hey, Bill, just for once I'd like for you to bring
in some women so we can have some intellectual
discourse.

DUNNISON: It's against camp regulations.

CALO: (*simultaneously*) ...camp regulations. Tell me,
Bill, what's on the menu today? Is it the fillet
mignon, or the beef Wellington? You know what I'd
like, some haggis.

DUNNISON: I don't think so. Vito, would you like to
come to my office?

VITO: What is it?

DUNNISON: It's rather private.

VITO: You could talk in front of these men. They're my
friends.

DUNNISON: I'd rather not.

VITO: Bill, please, faccimu i pirritu insieme.
[Bill, please, we fart together.]

DUNNISON: (*pause*) There's a letter for you. (*he hands the letter to VITO*) It came in yesterday. I thought you should know right away. (*VITO reads the letter. Pause.*) I'm sorry.

ROMANO: What happened?

CALO: Vito, speak to us.

VITO: (*pause*) My father is dead.

ROMANO: (*moves towards him*) Vito....

CALO: (*stops playing the mandolin*) I don't believe this.

LUCA: Will he be allowed to attend his father's funeral?

DUNNISON: He's already buried. I'm sorry.

VITO: (*pause*) He wanted to be buried in Italy, next to his mother. That was his wish. I promised him I would do that.

DUNNISON: If you like, you can write a letter immediately to your family. I'll see to it that it gets there promptly. I'm sorry, Vito.

VITO: That is not my name.

DUNNISON: Excuse me?

VITO: Vito is not my name. (*pause*) Vito is my father's name. My name is Antonio.

DUNNISON: What?

VITO: The day the RCMP came to arrest the Italians, they had a name on the list: Vito Di Napoli. My father. I was fixing the door, just as my father had told me to do. My father Vito was on his way from work. They asked me if I was Vito Di Napoli, and I said that I was.

DUNNISON: And you're not?

VITO: It was my father.

LUCA: They arrested the wrong man?

VITO: I'm young. My father has put in many years. I could spare a few. He can't.

DUNNISON: And you never told anyone?

VITO: Under the circumstances, what would you have done?

DUNNISON: My God.

ROMANO: Bill, this man must be released, the error is obvious. They have to let him go.

DUNNISON: I'll inform the Colonel immediately.

ROMANO: (*erupting*) You have to do more than inform him! This is outrageous! This man here, under the name that he's been arrested, does not exist. He should not be here. Give him his freedom!

DUNNISON: I'm but a minor link in the chain of command, Dicenzo! Now I respect the injustice....

ROMANO: Do you?

DUNNISON: Yes I do. But shouting in the hut here will not serve a thing. Now compose yourself. (*pause*) Antonio. May I offer my condolences. (*he crosses to VITO and hands him a pack of cigarettes*) I thought you might like this. You're a brave man. (*exits*)

> CALO *continues playing the mandolin.* LUCA *offers his hand to* VITO. ROMANO *embraces* VITO. VITO *is now crying.*

Scene 3

LUCERNE appears at his desk, DUNNISON enters.

LUCERNE: Stand easy.

DUNNISON: Sir. On the matter of Mr. Di Napoli. The man should be released. It is a blatant error. It is wrong to keep him here.

LUCERNE: I'm not running a summer camp here, Sergeant!

DUNNISON: Sir. By military standards, this is a very messy operation. Not the way the camp is run, sir. That standard is executed with extreme precision. It's the arrests themselves. Our government has not thought this through.

LUCERNE: Our country is at war.

DUNNISON: Yes, I realize that, sir. But with the exception of a few prisoners, a handful really, the prisoners aren't guilty of anything. They have no prior criminal records. Not one of them has been formally charged. They are here merely on suspicion. Ninety per cent of the Italian prisoners are Canadian citizens. People whom I swore to protect as a military man.

LUCERNE: Our government acted deliberately, but in light of the situation, there was no choice!

DUNNISON: They could've consulted with the military.

LUCERNE: That would just put tanks in the streets. And that is not what you want, now is it Sergeant?

DUNNISON: No, sir. Permission to speak, sir?

LUCERNE: Speak.

DUNNISON: I read their letters, sir, they write love letters. These people don't want to fight. What worries me is that at some point, the war will be over. If we lose, we've still imprisoned innocent men. If we win…. Well, Colonel, if we win…this country will have set a terrible precedent of prejudice. Of intolerance. We'll have to live with this. These people won't trust us anymore.

LUCERNE: (*pause, hands him a paper*) This is Di Napoli's release order. Execute it immediately.

DUNNISON: Yes, sir.

CALO enters.

CALO: You wanted to see me, sir?

LUCERNE: The General will be inspecting the camp by the end of the month. He happens to love opera. Can you put together some selections from *La Traviata*? It's his favourite opera.

CALO: Anything else?

LUCERNE: I trust your judgment in music.

CALO: Maybe something choral? We have the voices, sir.

LUCERNE: Fine then. I suggest you start rehearsing immediately. (*exits*)

CALO: We're just his puppets. He plays us like marionettes. It's not music anymore. It's work.

DUNNISON: You're lucky you even have instruments.

CALO: What's with you, Bill?

DUNNISON: I'm just trying to find out what this is all about. How does an artist and an intellectual like you become a Fascist?

CALO: I grew up in Italy. I saw Mussolini come into power. He came like a storm in the night. I was there. I saw it. People were hungry. They needed education. Before Mussolini, we had a King who didn't care. Now in the poor villages of Italy, the children don't pay for their school books. They are provided by the state. Mussolini did that; people were working, and proud to be Italian again.

DUNNISON: His ideology has created a world war. Can't you see why the government considers you a threat to the security of this country?

CALO: A threat? The promotion of Fascism in this country is not a threat.

DUNNISON: How can you say that?

CALO: There was never any talk of violence. Mussolini's views are now being questioned because of his alliance with Hitler. Who was to know that Italy would be involved in a war? The nations of Europe dismissed Italy as insignificant. What would this country do? Would it not fight back? Would it not demand respect? Forty years ago, there were hardly any churches in the Italian neighbourhoods of Toronto and Montréal. When I worked for the Italian Consulate, the funds that were provided by the Italian government...we allocated to the building of community centres and churches. Mussolini made sure we had a place to pray. What is wrong with that? All this war is proving is that he was not militarily prepared.

DUNNISON: It's doing more than that, Calo. Your Duce allied himself with one of the most terrifying and brutal dictators history has ever seen.

CALO: I know. (*pause*) We're both involved in the same deception, Bill. When the Italians were arrested in Toronto, they held us for a time at the Canadian

National Exhibition Grounds. They displayed us like cattle. People who were our friends—ate our pasta, wore our clothes and shoes, came to gather. They spat on us. They threw things at us. I thought this was a decent country. Is there not an assumption of innocence before being found guilty in your justice system? Why then did they parade us through the streets of Toronto? Why? Shit was thrown on me. It was washed away with piss. This I was told was a civilized society. Yes, Bill. I am proud to be an Italian. No. I am not dangerous. Yes, I worked for The Fascist Party. And I love this country.

DUNNISON: How do you explain the millions who are dying?

CALO: I don't know, Bill! Can't you see this is tearing me apart?

Scene 4

M. BEAUCHAMP appears waiting. HÉLÈNE enters.

M. BEAUCHAMP: Où est-ce que t'étais?
[Where were you?]

HÉLÈNE: Je suis allée à la pharmacie, comme vous me l'avez demandé.
[I went to the pharmacy, just as you told me to.]

M. BEAUCHAMP: Je suis supposer de manger quand? Je travaille toute la journée au marché. Le moindre des choses c'est d'avoir mon repas quand je rentre.
[When am I supposed to eat? I work all day at the store. The least I can expect when I get home is my dinner.]

HÉLÈNE: Je suis allée voir des amis. Votre repas est prêt. J'ai juste à le réchauffer.

[I went to see some friends. Your dinner is ready. I just have to heat it up.]

M. BEAUCHAMP: Alors, c'est prêt?

[So, it's ready?]

HÉLÈNE: Oui.

[Yes.]

M. BEAUCHAMP: Alors, tu l'a préparé à l'avance. (*pause*) Comme ça, ça te donne plus de temps d'aller voir les Dicenzo.

[So, you already prepared it. That way, it gives you more time to go see the Dicenzos.]

HÉLÈNE: J'étais avec Giselle.

[I was with Giselle.]

M. BEAUCHAMP: (*suddenly with fury*) Menteuse! Je suis ton père! Sais-tu qu'est-ce que c'est de savoir que tous mes amis me parlent dans le dos? Que ma fille sort avec cette espèce d'Italien? Sais-tu dans quelle situation tu me mets?

[Liar! I'm your father! Do you know what it's like to have my friends talk behind my back? That my daughter is going out with an Italian? I've heard it all day. Do you know the situation you've put me in?]

HÉLÈNE: Et moi? Et mes émotions? Ça compte pour rien?

[And me? What about my feelings? Don't they count for anything?]

M. BEAUCHAMP: Tes émotions ne me concernent pas. Tout ce qui me concerne, c'est ma réputation! Tu vois pas ce que cet homme-là est en train de faire? Il abuse de ta bonne volonté.

[Your feelings don't concern me. What concerns me, is my reputation! Can't you see what this man is doing to you? He's taking advantage of you.]

HÉLÈNE: Comment vous pouvez dire ça? Vous le connaissez même pas. Si vous saviez comme il est doux. C'est l'homme le plus brave et le plus honorable que j'ai jamais rencontré. Tous ce qu'il fait, c'est protéger le bien-être de Maria.

[How can you say that? You don't even know him. If only you knew how gentle he is. He's the bravest, most honourable man I've ever met. Everything he does, he does to protect Maria.]

M. BEAUCHAMP: Es-tu amoureuse de lui?

[Are you in love with him?]

HÉLÈNE: Papa.

M. BEAUCHAMP: Réponds!

[Answer me!]

HÉLÈNE: (*exploding*) Oui! Je suis amoureuse de lui! Je l'aime! Je l'adore! C'est l'homme de ma vie!

[Yes! I'm in love with him! I love him! I adore him! He's the man of my dreams!]

M. BEAUCHAMP: As-tu couché avec lui?

[Have you slept with him?]

HÉLÈNE: Papa.

M. BEAUCHAMP: AS-TU COUCHÉ AVEC LUI?

[HAVE YOU SLEPT WITH HIM?]

HÉLÈNE: OUI! On fait l'amour chaque fois qu'on peut.

[YES! We make love every chance we get.]

M. BEAUCHAMP: (*slaps her*) Salope! T'es devenue une vulgaire putain. À cause d'une espèce d'Italien onctueuse qui jette son charme souriant de gangster! Tu m'as trahie, tu as trahie la mémoire de ta mère, tu as trahie tes amis, et ta patrie! Une fille qui j'ai tant aimé.

[You whore! You've become a vulgar little whore. All because of an oily Italian who flashes his smiling gangster charm! You've betrayed me, you've betrayed the memory of your mother, you've betrayed your friends and your country! A daughter whom I loved so much.]

HÉLÈNE: Comment vous pouvez dire que vous m'aimez, et me traiter de cette façon-là? Je suis une femme, papa. J'ai trente-quatre ans! Regardez moi! Je ne suis plus votre petite fille. La vie passe à côté de moi. Parce que je suis obligée de prendre soins de vous. J'ai travaillé au magasin toute ma vie, j'ai sacrifié ma jeunesse. Vous avez-vous seulement demandé si j'avais des besoins, moi? Non. J'ai pris soins de vous, c'est tout. Et pour une fois que je demande quelque chose pour moi, vous m'abandonnez. Vous êtes vieux, papa. Moi je suis jeune, j'ai la vie devant moi, et vous m'empêcherez pas de la vivre.

[How can you say you love me, and then treat me this way? I'm a woman, papa. I'm thirty-four years old! Look at me! I'm not your little girl anymore. Life is passing me by. Because I've had to take care of you. I've worked at the store all my life, I've sacrificed my youth. Have you ever once asked about my needs? No. I've taken care of you. And now for the first time that I've asked something for myself, you abandon me. You're old, papa. I'm young, I have my life in front of me, and you can't stop me from living it.]

M. BEAUCHAMP: Ingrate! Tu oses me parler ainsi! Qu'est-ce qui te donne le droit? Pour qui tu te prends?
[You spiteful little brat! How dare you talk to me like that! Who gave you the right? Who do you think you are?]

HÉLÈNE: Papa. Pourquoi? Je ne peux plus vivre comme ça. Je ne peux pas. Je ne vous reconnais plus. Je regrette. Je vais vivre avec mon homme à mes conditions. Et vous ne pourrez rien faire. Parce que je vous quitte. Comme ça vous pourrez vivre sans être gêné par la présence d'une fille honteuse. Mais moi, j'aurai ma dignité. J'aurai ma vie! (*exits*)
[Papa. Why are you doing this? I can't live like this anymore. I just can't. I don't know you anymore. I'm sorry. I'll be with my man, how I want. And you can't do anything. Because I'm leaving. That way, you can live without the presence of a shameful daughter. But I'll have my dignity. I'll have my life!]

M. BEAUCHAMP: Hélène! Reviens! S'il te plaît, reviens! (*he breaks down*)
[Hélène! Come back! Please, come back!]

Scene 5

CENZO is waiting at a street corner, HÉLÈNE enters.

CENZO: What took you so long? Did anyone follow you?

HÉLÈNE: Let's leave right now. I made arrangements with my cousin. He's coming to pick us up. We can be in Quebec City by tonight. We'll start all over. Let's go.

CENZO: Hélène….

HÉLÈNE: I can't live this life anymore. I can't. Please do this for me.

CENZO: Not now.

HÉLÈNE: My father knows about us. Somebody told him. I know my father, he'll get you arrested, he will. And he'll ruin me.

CENZO: Your father is bluffing.

HÉLÈNE: He isn't. I'm his only daughter. I have to leave!

CENZO: Hélène, please, don't do this to me. Please. I beg you. I need you.

HÉLÈNE: I have no choice!

CENZO: Hélène....

HÉLÈNE: You'll never find the informer! Whoever it was is probably gone. You're obsessed with this search. Look what it's doing to us. To me.

CENZO: Hélène. I'm nothing without you. I have no life without you. I'd rather just throw myself in the river.

HÉLÈNE: (*slaps him*) Don't you talk to me like that! Now compose yourself! (*pause*) I have no more home. Comprends-tu? I've left everything.

Scene 6

The Barracks Hut. June 22, 1942. LUCERNE appears, inspecting the hut. LUCA enters.

LUCA: I'm sorry, Colonel. I'll wait outside.

LUCERNE: Stay. (*pause*) Why aren't you with the other men?

LUCA: I came to get a pack of cigarettes.

LUCERNE: Sit. You want to get out of here, Luca? (*pause*) Let's take the gloves off, shall we? I don't like disruptions under my command. Now according to your letters, you have a daughter. Rosetta. You think she misses her daddy? Does she work for your organization?

LUCA: I'm a truck driver. I'm in the delivery business.

LUCERNE: What is it you deliver?

LUCA: It depends on the contract: meat, clothes, automotive parts, cigarettes. Whatever.

LUCERNE: Have you ever delivered for Rocco Perri?

LUCA: I never heard of the name. Who is he?

LUCERNE: Maybe you can tell me. He lives in Barracks No. 8. In your file, there are financial statements which claim that you exported goods across the U.S. border for a Donato Pileggi. Mr. Pileggi is a secretary in Rocco Perri's organization. You claim to have no knowledge of this?

LUCA: Like I said, I just deliver the goods. Who knows where it's coming from, you know what I mean?

LUCERNE: Are you a member of the Cosa Nostra?

LUCA: The what?

LUCERNE: You heard me.

LUCA: Never heard of it.

LUCERNE: What are your views on Benito Mussolini?

LUCA: That son-of-a-bitch—excuse my language, but right now, in front of you, if he were here in my presence, I'd cut out his throat, and watch him eat it. Then I'd take his balls—excuse me, you have to let me be myself...and he would have them for dessert.

LUCERNE: So you don't like him?

LUCA: In a manner of speaking. You know, Colonel, I would like to say that these arrests, in my opinion, were totally justified. Fascists are not to be trusted. They come in as Socialists, but they're just cleverly disguised businessmen wrapped tightly around a loaded gun. Canada must be protected. I just wish that the authorities were a little more careful in who they arrested. Don't you think?

LUCERNE: You'll never get out of here, Luca. You'll have your day in front of the judge. And he'll see right through your facade. Is this what you were looking for? (*shows him his dagger*) Quite an object. You threaten one more man in this camp, you undermine my order here one more time, I'll have your sorry ass in solitary confinement for a year. Got that?

CALO: (*entering*) Orchestra is ready, sir. A little send off for the men.

LUCERNE: Has the truck arrived?

CALO: It just pulled in.

LUCERNE exits, as ROMANO and VITO enter.

VITO: (*entering*) Well this is it, guys. I came to say goodbye. (*he hugs CALO*) Calo, keep that orchestra alive, the men need it. We'll see each other again. Romano, I'll see you in Montréal. I was honoured to serve with you. You're a good man. I'll be waiting for you in Montréal. (*hugs him, turns to LUCA*) Luca, take care of yourself. (*he rips up a piece of paper*) They want me to join the army. I already fought my war.

CALO: You better get going, you don't want to miss that train.

LUCERNE enters the hut.

LUCERNE: Stand easy, men. Di Napoli, Antonio. My final instructions to you are to get straight to work. It's the only way you can help yourself, your family, and your country.

VITO: My country? Do I have one?

LUCERNE: That is your decision.

DUNNISON enters the hut.

DUNNISON: Colonel Lucerne. You are requested at the office, sir. Wire just came in. Tobruk has just fallen to the Germans.

LUCERNE: (*pause*) Alright. Let's get back to work. Di Napoli, goodbye, and God-speed. (*exits*)

DUNNISON: You better hop to it. The truck is ready to move out. You got your ticket?

VITO: Yes.

DUNNISON: Well. Good luck. (*exits*)

VITO: Is Tobruk important?

LUCA: It means The Allies don't have Africa yet. This war is never going to end.

ROMANO: (*hands a letter to VITO*) Give this to my wife.

VITO: I will. (*turns to Luca*) Good luck. (*exits*)

LUCA: There's no stopping the Germans. We're all dead in here, do you understand? Dead! He wants the world. He's got it. And what do you think they'll do to us? You think the Canadian Army is going to spend time looking after a bunch of heart-broken Italian men? They'll shoot us all, and get it over with.

CALO: I can't believe it. Germany has Africa.

ROMANO: They're releasing men every month.

CALO: But not all of us.

LUCA: You're the last guy they'll want to let go. A Fascist?

ROMANO: The system is working here, come on guys!

CALO: Romano, the tide of the war has not shifted yet. Don't you understand? Prison camps are still going to be a top priority for security reasons.

ROMANO: You'll have your day in front of the judge.

LUCA: This changes everything. What's the matter with you?

ROMANO: Just give it some time.

LUCA: You really are something, you really put value into this stuff. You think the men in this camp could give a shit about your honour code? You live in a fantasy world.

ROMANO: The reality here, Luca, is that we have no choice!

LUCA: Yes we do!

ROMANO: (*pause*) You talking about an escape? Is that what this is about? Go ahead, Luca, try it. You'll get nowhere. Those Frenchmen that broke out were caught within hours. Who are you kidding?

LUCA: At least they tried.

ROMANO: You're really thinking about this. What is the matter with you? There is a big difference with a Frenchman escaping and an Italian. Killing a Frenchman from Quebec could spark a civil war. Killing an Italian will mean nothing to them. You'll make it worse for all of us.

LUCA: I've heard enough.

ROMANO: You've been fighting me from the very start. You've had your ways in the camp, you set up your gang, you controlled the trade...but this one you can't win.

LUCA: I will not die without my freedom.

ROMANO: Alright. You do what you have to do, and I'll do what I have to do.

LUCA: What does that mean? (*pause*) What do you mean by that? (*pause*) You wouldn't dare do what you're thinking. You have no spine. You sicken me. You actually believe in this country. Look what they've done to you. You've been dancing with the Colonel, you've played his game, and now what? You're a joke, Romano. A big stupid fucking joke. Go ahead, play with them, my conscience is clear. (*exits*)

CALO: He's a hothead. You just can't reason with him. He wants to break out, let him do it. It's his life. (*pause*) There's nothing you can do about this.

ROMANO: Is that what the men think of me?

CALO: Don't listen to him. I grew up with men like that. (*pause*) Don't do it. (*pause*) Don't tell the Colonel. You'll regret it.

ROMANO: It could endanger us.

CALO: You don't know that.

ROMANO: I know the rules. Lucerne will come down hard. I have a wife.

CALO: Romano, listen to me. The most Lucerne will do to us, is take away our instruments. Maybe this whole hut will go into solitary confinement. And maybe Luca will get shot. If you tell, they'll know it was you. You'll have to live with your conscience the

rest of your life. Luca isn't worth it. (*ROMANO exits*)
Romano! Romano! Listen to me! (*runs out after him*)

Scene 7

The Camp Office. LUCERNE and DUNNISON
appear surrounding ROMANO who is seated.

LUCERNE: You have something to report?

ROMANO: Yes, sir. (*pause*) The road is complete.

LUCERNE: (*pause*) Good job, Dicenzo. New detail for
tomorrow, all men are required for duty in the
camp. The General is due for an inspection, and I
need it in tip-top shape. Is that clear? I mean
cleaner than it's ever been. You inform the hut
leaders of the importance of this inspection. I'm
waiting for the order to come in.

ROMANO: The order, sir?

LUCERNE: Petawawa is being shut down. Military
operations will resume immediately.

ROMANO: Does that mean we're being sent home?

DUNNISON: What it means, is that the prisoners will
be transferred to Gagetown, New Brunswick. The
order for the detaining of prisoners is still in effect.

ROMANO: I see. I was wondering, the judge in
Pembroke…he recommended me for release. Any
news yet on when I'm going home?

LUCERNE: (*pause*) You haven't told him?

DUNNISON: (*pause*) The judge did recommend your
release.

ROMANO: So what's the problem?

DUNNISON: Your release has been denied. The Minister of Justice still considers you a threat.

LUCERNE: You have enemies, Dicenzo, and they go real high up. Someone up there doesn't like you. You'll have to try again. That will be all. (*pause*) That will be all, Romano.

ROMANO: What does your government want from me? I'm a construction man. Why am I considered a threat?

LUCERNE: You're asking the wrong man, Dicenzo.

ROMANO: Am I? What did they teach you in your Military School? Not to think for yourself?

LUCERNE: Dunnison. Leave the room.

DUNNISON: Sir....

LUCERNE: Leave the room. Now!

ROMANO: Stay! What are you afraid of Lucerne? Maybe this good soldier will have an opinion?

LUCERNE: His opinion doesn't count.

ROMANO: You hear that, Bill. You're just part of the machinery.

DUNNISON: Permission to speak, sir?

LUCERNE: Permission denied, leave!

DUNNISON: Permission to speak, sir?

LUCERNE: Permission denied!

DUNNISON: Sir! I will remind you that this man here is a civilian!

LUCERNE: You are bordering on insubordination, soldier! Now leave the fucking room!

ROMANO: I charge you with insubordination! I'M A CANADIAN CITIZEN! I'VE PAID MY TAXES

WHICH MAKE THE GOVERNMENT RUN! You will listen to me! I'VE DONE NOTHING WRONG! You can't treat people like this! The government is asking the prisoners who are being released to go fight in the Canadian Army. There is something wrong there! THIS COUNTRY COULD KISS MY ASS!

DUNNISON: (*calmly goes to ROMANO*) Let's go, Romano.

ROMANO: What more do you want from me, Lucerne? You want me to keep playing your game?

DUNNISON: ...let's go....

LUCERNE: Wait! Remove your hands from the prisoner, soldier. (*DUNNISON does so*) What do you mean by that? Keep playing my game?

ROMANO: Nothing.

LUCERNE: You had something to tell me, tell me now. (*pause*) I presume you would like to see your daughter at some point. Yes, Dicenzo, I know of your heartache, I know what family means to you. Now, you had something to tell me.

ROMANO: A breach of security, sir. One of the men...there is talk...a plan.... I'm not sure of the details...

LUCERNE: I need a name.

ROMANO: Sir. I can't say for sure...it's a group of men...it includes the French.

LUCERNE: Names, Dicenzo!

ROMANO: Sir. I need your assurances....

LUCERNE: Let's get one thing straight. I can go right to the Minister of Justice himself and tell him that you just reported an attempted escape. It will mean nothing. Do you understand? You are in the middle of a military operation. Security is imperative. If you hold up this conversation for one more second, I will classify this camp as a hostile military zone. That means war. That means guns will fire. Men will die. It's your choice.

ROMANO: Luca Delferro.

LUCERNE: The Sicilian?

ROMANO: Yes.

LUCERNE: You just informed on one of your own.

ROMANO: For the good of the others, sir.

LUCERNE: What are you made of, Dicenzo?

ROMANO: There is no reason to mock me, sir. I'm doing my job as ordered.

LUCERNE: It isn't mockery, Dicenzo, it's astonishment.

The phone rings.

DUNNISON: (*on phone*) Sergeant Dunnison. Yes. Uh huh. Right. I'll tell him. (*hangs up*) Sir, the order came in. Camp Petawawa is to be closed. Commence immediate transfer of prisoners after the General's inspection.

LUCERNE: Right.

ROMANO: Could you make him run for a bit, sir?

LUCERNE: Run? He'll have no place to go.

ROMANO: It's for my own safety. If you let him run for a bit, he won't think he was informed upon. I'm asking as a favour.

LUCERNE: (*pause*) Bring the prisoner back to his hut. (*pause*) And report to me at 1600 hours. Soldier. (*exits*)

DUNNISON: Yes sir. (*pause*)

ROMANO: Help me, Bill, help me. I don't know what I've just done.

Scene 8

M. LEFEBVRE is at his office. CENZO and LORENZO enter.

CENZO: I'm glad you made this time for me.

LEFEBVRE: (*he sees LORENZO*) I don't want that man in this office.

CENZO: I'm here for my brother.

LEFEBVRE: You understand, there is attorney client privilege.

CENZO: So I take it the RCMP has not asked to see your files concerning Romano?

LEFEBVRE: (*pause*) Will you get to the point?

CENZO: Lorenzo here, as you know, put a down payment on a house that was yet to be built. Money that he may never see again.

LEFEBVRE: He will see his money again. I promise you that.

LORENZO: Cha detto?
[What did he say?]

LEFEBVRE: On va récoupérer votre argent, Lorenzo, j'en suis sûr.
[We'll get your money back, Lorenzo, I'm sure of it.]

LORENZO: Ah, bene, bene. Cha detto?
[Ah, good, good. What did he say?]

CENZO: Ascolta. So, Lorenzo was one of over a dozen men who made these down payments. Am I right?

LEFEBVRE: Correct.

CENZO: What happened to all this money?

LEFEBVRE: Under the Defence Of Canada Regulations, Italians are not able to purchase any land or houses without express written authorization from the proper authorities.

CENZO: And the money?

LEFEBVRE: It's frozen. There's nothing that can be done until the regulations are lifted.

CENZO: Okay. That much I understand. What about Romano's land purchase?

LEFEBVRE: I'm not at liberty to discuss that.

CENZO: This man here is from the old country. He doesn't know new law. He knows old law. Primal. You hurt me, I hurt you back. This man's future has been destroyed. I don't know how much longer I can hold him back. He's talking vengeance on Guido Lombardo. He'll get himself killed.

LORENZO: Missyou Lefebvre, guarda cha. (*shows him a photo*) Questo e mio figlio. My son. I no see him for two years. They take him to Petawawa. My business…is ruinato. Io mo non ho niente. Mi hanno riduttu propio come nu cane.
[Mister Lefebvre, look here. This is my son. I haven't seen him in two years. They took him to Petawawa. My business is ruined. Now, I have nothing. They've reduced me to the level of a dog.]

LEFEBVRE: (*pause*) What do you want to know?

CENZO: I know you went to the auction. Who bought the land?

LEFEBVRE: (*pause*) I went. The bids placed were so low…. I mean they were auctioning off Italian properties and possessions for virtually pennies. In half a day, I saw all of what Italian Canadians built thrown right into the wind. I could not believe my eyes. Then came the bid for the land in LaSalle…. I…you see…. Based on Romano's plans, in ten years, he would've been the biggest, if not the biggest in the country. When you're that size, you're open to criticism from all over. But something I… that day—Look, there's nothing I can do to help you.

CENZO: Someone destroyed my brother's business. You're his lawyer. Unless they kill my brother, he will be released, and we will start all over again. I can't do that unless I know who's in my way. Now, you were about to recall something.

LEFEBVRE: Listen. I will go this far and no further. Guido Lombardo is just a front man…to deter attention from the Government…. Do you understand?

CENZO: Someone was doing Lombardo's dirty work. Who was it?

LORENZO: Missyou Lefebvre… if you no tell me… maybe you no walk so good no more. E pu cantamu!
[Mister Lefebvre, if you don't tell me, maybe you won't walk so good anymore. And then we'll sing!]

CENZO: Mr. Lefebvre, you know who this man is. I can see it in your face. Okay: See this pen on your desk? I'll tell you what. (*takes the pen*) I'm going to place the pen right here at the corner of the desk. See? I'm going to ask you a question. And then I'm going to turn around. If you move the pen, then the answer to my question is yes. If you don't move the pen, the answer is no. Nothing was said. Nothing was betrayed. You said nothing, so no one can hold you to it. Your client attorney privilege will be intact. Okay? (*pause*) This Guido Lombardo…did

he know Bruno Benevento, Maria's cousin?
Andiamo, Lorenzo, gli affari qui sono finiti.
[Let's go Lorenzo. Our business here is done.]

*CENZO and LORENZO rise and turn away from
LEFEBVRE. LEFEBVRE takes the pen and places it
in his jacket. He's answered the question. CENZO
turns to see that the pen is no longer there.*

CENZO: Thank you, Mr. Lefebvre. You will never see
me again. Thank you. (*to Lorenzo*) Andiamo, hai
fatto bene, molto bene.
[Let's go, you've done well, very well.]

LORENZO: Speriamo che tutto e apposto. Allora, fu
Bruno?
[I hope everything went well. So, it was Bruno?]

CENZO: Si.

LORENZO: Quel figliu di puttana. (*CENZO whispers in
his ear. They exit.*)
[That son of a whore.]

Scene 9

*The MAN who attacked MARIA appears. He is
talking to someone.*

MAN 1: Hey! Hey, man, are you here? I can't see you.

BRUNO: (*appears from the shadows*) I told you never to
come here.

MAN 1: I'm being paid good money to do my job, now
you better do yours. Guido Lombardo needs this
Cenzo guy arrested. If you don't do it, he'll waste
him.

BRUNO: He's untouchable, he's never in the same
place twice.

MAN 1: If you don't take care of it, he'll take care of you.

BRUNO: Look, I'm in deep enough as it is. There's nothing more I can do.

MAN 1: Then I'll take care of it.

BRUNO: Like you took care of my cousin? You were supposed to just scare her.

MAN 1: Hey, man, she had it coming! (*BRUNO lunges at him, but he secures BRUNO in an arm lock*) Don't you try that shit with me. You fucking guineas are all the same. You say one thing, you do something else. You do as you're told, or Mr. Lombardo will spill the whole can of worms. (*lets him go and exits*)

> *LORENZO appears in the middle of a street. BRUNO hides.*

LORENZO: (*to the neighbourhood*) BRUNO BENEVENTO! Mi stai ascoltando! Sei tu il tradditore! Perche l'hai fatto? Brutto schiffozzo! Tu devi pagare per quello che hai fatto! Tu pagi chu la tua vita! Capisce paesano! Chu la tua vita! BRUNO BENEVENTO! Tu sarai servito in purgatorio! Il tuo maestro e proprio il diavolo! Madame e Missyous, l'homme qui s'appele Bruno Benevento est un uomo di merde! To the eenglish people: Bruno Benevento is the son of a goat! He kill the life of Romano Dicenzo!

[BRUNO BENEVENTO! Do you hear me! You are the traitor! Why did you do it? You disgusting bastard! You have to pay for what you've done! You will pay with your life! You understand! With your life! BRUNO BENEVENTO! You will be served in hell! You master is the devil himself! Ladies and gentlemen, the man who is named Bruno Benevento is full of shit! To the English people: Bruno Benevento is the son of a goat! He killed the life of Romano Dicenzo!]

HÉLÈNE comes running in.

HÉLÈNE: Lorenzo, qu'est-ce que tu fais? Tu peux pas crier comme ça dans la rue, c'est pas normal!
[Lorenzo, what are you doing? You can't scream in the street like that, it's not normal.]

LORENZO: Mademoiselle Beauchamp, moi je travaille comme je veux. Non mi comminciari a scaciare li palli cha cu nu pugnu vi mandu tutti sopra a luna!
[Miss Beauchamp, I do things my way. Don't start busting my balls, because I'll start throwing punches and I'll send everyone to the moon!]

HÉLÈNE: Andiamo a casa.
[Let's go home.]

LORENZO: (*to the neighbourhood*) Bruno Benevento, fatti vedere a faccia!
[Bruno Benevento, show your face!]

HÉLÈNE: …andiamo…andiamo…. (*they exit*)

BRUNO re-enters, he looks around. MAN 2 enters.

MAN 2: Where are you going?

BRUNO: Leave me alone.

MAN 2: Come with me.

BRUNO: No.

MAN 2: You'll be safe. Trust me.

CENZO enters.

CENZO: Let him go. (*pause*) You have witnesses here. This is a family thing.

MARIA and HÉLÈNE enter with LORENZO, who is carrying a piece of wood.

LORENZO: Allora. A festa e comminciata? Mo ti rumpo a cappu!
[Alright now. The party has begun? I'm going to break your head!]

MAN 2: Alright. Take it easy. (*he looks at BRUNO, then exits*)

BRUNO turns around to face MARIA.

MARIA: What did you do?

CENZO: (*pause*) My brother. You have to answer for my brother.

BRUNO: Maria…Maria…listen…. I'm your cousin….

LORENZO: A cussi si trattanu le cugini?
[This is the way you treat your cousins?]

BRUNO: It's not like that, Maria.

CENZO: They transferred Romano to another prison camp. Petawawa has been closed. Men have been released. BUT NOT MY BROTHER!

BRUNO: I'm being accused here of something I didn't do.

CENZO: You couldn't get a partnership with Dicenzo Construction, Guido Lombardo approached you with an offer. What did he give you?

BRUNO: This guy has some imagination…. I don't even know him….

CENZO: ENOUGH OF THESE LIES! You accused my brother!

BRUNO: I didn't accuse anyone! I'm the one who's being accused here. Where's the proof? What do you think this is? You think we're back home, Cenzo? You want to have some justice in the streets? Go ahead, kill me! You have no proof!

CENZO: I don't need proof.

BRUNO: Then you have nothing.

CENZO: (*he grabs him suddenly and pulls his knife to his throat*) You start talking or I'll kill you right now.

LORENZO: Mo cantamu, Bruno.
[Now we'll sing, Bruno.]

MARIA: Cenzo, put that down!

HÉLÈNE: (*overlapping*) Cenzo, please!

CENZO: Stay away from me, all of you. I don't care anymore! I've been running around for two years like a dog, I have nothing to lose. Start talking or I'll kill you!

BRUNO: Please....

CENZO: Why did you do it?

BRUNO: Listen....

CENZO: I'm giving you one more second.

BRUNO: You don't know what you're talking about.... (*CENZO cuts his cheek*) Okay, okay! (*CENZO lets him go, BRUNO is bleeding*) It's Lombardo! It was all Guido Lombardo! He couldn't compete with Romano. Romano pushed me aside.... I meant nothing to him. NOTHING! Lombardo offered me a partnership in his company. He needed Romano out of the way. He needed an accusation. The RCMP came to me...I gave them an accusation. I told them Romano was a Fascist.

MARIA: Why did you do that?

BRUNO: I didn't think they'd put him in a war camp. I never thought it would've gone to that. I thought they were just going to question him...to slow down the company....

CENZO: And you believed that?

BRUNO: Romano should've listened to me! I have my own family to feed! I was led to believe that I was going to be a part of Dicenzo Construction.... Lombardo gave me an opportunity.... It's called competition, Cenzo! SON OF A BITCH! I accused Romano. And I still accuse him. For being a greedy self-serving peasant! He wants to act like a prince, he's just a common ignorant fucking peasant! You hear me?

CENZO: (*he runs at him to bring home the knife, but MARIA steps in the way*) Let me through, Maria, this is man to man.

MARIA: No.

CENZO: Maria....

MARIA: NO!

BRUNO: (*crying*) I thought it was harmless...I thought it was harmless....

MARIA: You will never speak my name. You will never set eyes on my child again. I never want to see you again. As of this day, my little Chiara has no uncle. You are nothing to me. Nothing. You destroyed my life when you accused Romano. As of this moment you have no family. You must now speak to God.

BRUNO: ...Maria....

MARIA: Get out of here!

BRUNO: ...Maria...please....

MARIA: Now!

> BRUNO exits. MARIA turns to CENZO, HÉLÈNE and LORENZO. Over this we hear the evening news over the sound system.

RADIO ANNOUNCER: Good evening, we interrupt our broadcast with this special news bulletin for May 7th 1945. Germany has just surrendered, the war in Europe is over. The surrender was unconditional. The Allies have succeeded in occupying the western part of Berlin, as the Russians control the eastern part. Negotiations will soon get underway as to setting up a judicial process for dealing with recent war crimes discovered by the Allies. Once again, the war in Europe is over. Germany has unconditionally surrendered.

Scene 10

The lights appear on ROMANO and CALO who stand about with their duffel bags. Gagetown, New Brunswick. Camp compound.

CALO: We did it. (*pause*) Where you going? (*pause*) Right. Where am I going?

ROMANO: Come with me. The train will stop in Montréal. Meet my family.

CALO: I need some time.

ROMANO: I understand.

CALO: (*pause*) I don't know what to do. I...I can't face my family. I came here a Fascist.... I thought it was the right thing to believe in.... I don't know who I am anymore.

ROMANO: You're an Italian. You have centuries of tradition behind you. This is not the time for a soft heart. Your family needs you now more than ever. Walk with that. You have your art. Your music. That is important.

CALO: I don't know....

ROMANO: Listen to me…this prison camp didn't defeat you. Don't let freedom defeat you. Walk proud, do you hear me! Tall! You are a Calabrese! Make your people proud. Let them know. Tell all your friends, your family, your children what happened to us. Let this feed you. Move ahead. It's the only way. If you're worried about work, come with me. I have houses to build. Do you understand? Look at me.

CALO: (*crying*) Romano….

ROMANO: My friend. My good good friend. Don't turn back now.

DUNNISON enters holding a mandolin.

DUNNISON: The trucks are ready. This is the last hut. You ready, Dicenzo?

ROMANO: Yes.

DUNNISON: Calo. I thought you might want to have this. (*gives him the mandolin*) I don't know what the army has in mind, but…what the hell…it's just music.

CALO: Thanks.

A honking is heard.

DUNNISON: You better get moving.

CALO: (*turns to ROMANO*) Thanks. (*turns to DUNNISON*) What about the other musicians?

DUNNISON: I made sure you're all on the same bus.

CALO: (*turns to ROMANO*) Good luck. (*exits*)

ROMANO: Play it loud, Calo! Loud and proud! You hear me? Calo!

DUNNISON: (*pause*) It's time, Dicenzo.

ROMANO: (*pause*) Yes.

DUNNISON: (*pause*) You served with honour, Romano, never forget that. (*pause*) What you did, you did for the good of the men. You're leaving here with your head held high. You did not become an informer, but a leader of men. Remember that. (*hands him a letter*) My last detail here. It's from your wife.

ROMANO: It's not opened.

DUNNISON: No. I didn't censor it. It's between man and wife. It isn't any of my business.

ROMANO: Thanks. Where are you off to?

DUNNISON: My life is the military. I go where I'm assigned.

ROMANO: And family?

DUNNISON: I have a woman waiting for me.

ROMANO: Yes. That's good. Well. Good luck. (*begins to go*)

DUNNISON: Romano....

ROMANO: Yes.

DUNNISON: (*salutes him*) Dio ti benedica! (*exits*)
[God bless you!]

> *ROMANO looks at the letter. We hear the Mandolin Orchestra playing.*

Scene 11

The lights appear in the backyard. June, 1945. MARIA is sewing the hem on a pair of pants. ROMANO enters with a duffel bag. MARIA continues sewing. He gently drops his bag. MARIA seems to feel his presence. She seems almost afraid to look back. ROMANO is frozen by the sight of her. MARIA finally puts her sewing down, and turns towards him. ROMANO tries to utter something, but he can't talk. He cries. MARIA moves towards him and caresses him ever so gently.

MARIA: Sshhh. I'm here now. I'm here. (*pause*) Come meet your little girl. (*they exit*)

Scene 12

October, 1945. The backyard. CENZO, HÉLÈNE, LORENZO and VITO appear in the backyard. ROMANO and MARIA enter.

LORENZO: Buon giorno. Vi saluto a tutti. Siete state veramente bravi. Tutti. Pero, la mia vita non e qui. Ritorno in Italia. Stu paese non e buono per me. (*to HÉLÈNE*) Mademoiselle Beauchamp, sei stata brava con me. Ti ringrazio, e tante belle cose. (*she embraces him*) Ah! Questo si, questo si. Un abbraccio si. [Good morning. I want to salute you all. You've all been very good to me. All of you. But, my life is not here. I'm returning to Italy. This country is not good for me. Miss Beauchamp, you've been very kind to me. I thank you, and I wish you all the best. Ah! This yes, this yes. A hug yes.]

HÉLÈNE: Lorenzo, I'm going to miss you. Sei un uomo molto gentile. Très gentil.

LORENZO: Merci. (*he turns to ROMANO*) Romano, buona fortuna. (*they embrace*) Sempre in gamba. Corragio!
[Thank you. Romano, good luck. Stay strong and healthy. Courage!]

ROMANO: Grazie.

LORENZO: Cenzo, io non ti scordo mai. E si venite in Italia, mi passa una visita.
[Cenzo, I will never forget you. If you come to Italy, come visit me.]

CENZO: Sarai servito. (*they embrace*)
[You will be served.]

LORENZO: Vito, la strada e sempre diritta! (*they embrace*)
[Vito, the road is always straight ahead!]

VITO: Ciao.

LORENZO: Maria...Maria.... (*he breaks down, she goes to him*) Dio ti benedica! Dio ti benedica! La tua piccirella, la devi proteggere.... Maria...io non ti scurdo mai. Mai. Venitemi a visitare. Teresina sarrebbe contenta. (*they embrace*) Ciao. (*exits*)
[Maria, Maria. God will bless you! God will bless you! You must protect your little child. Maria, I will never forget you. Never. Come visit me. Teresina would be happy. Goodbye.]

VITO: Poor man.

CENZO: He's probably doing the right thing, going back to Italy.

MARIA: I'll miss him. He's a good man.

HÉLÈNE: He came a long way just to go home again. (*CENZO crosses to her*) What time will you be back tonight?

CENZO: I don't know. We're pouring the foundation today.

VITO: The cement trucks should be there in an hour. We should get going.

CENZO: Let's say around six.

HÉLÈNE: I'll be waiting.

VITO: So. Romano, what do you say?

ROMANO: (*long pause, looks at MARIA*) Let's get back to work.

The lights fade slowly to black.

THE END

Facts Regarding the Historical Context of the Play

On September 1, 1939, Germany invaded Poland, igniting World War II.

On September 3, 1939, the Government of Canada issued the *Defence Of Canada Regulations*. The purpose of the Regulations was to give the government of Prime Minister Mackenzie King full authority to destroy any sign of subversion in time of war. The Minister of Justice was thus fully empowered to arraign, arrest, and question any individual and suspend any and all rights of that individual should he or she be regarded even with suspicion.

What this action did was to immediately create a different class of citizens. Those citizens came to be known as "Enemy Aliens."

With the *Defence Of Canada Regulations* now intact, the Royal Canadian Mounted Police, provincial and local police forces were all now empowered to collect lists of names of people they deemed to be dangerous to the welfare of the state: suspected fifth columnists, Fascists, Communists, anarchists, etc., were listed as possible suspects. No proof was needed. No trial was necessary.

On June 8, 1940, President Roosevelt gave a speech which was universally interpreted as a last warning to Italian Dictator Benito Mussolini.

On June 10, 1940, not heeding Roosevelt's or Churchill's warnings, Mussolini entered World War II on the side of Germany by declaring war against England and France. In support of England, Canada declared war on Italy. That day, the arrests in Canada began. Six thousand Canadian men of Italian origin were ticketed as enemy aliens. Most of these were Canadian-born citizens.

Of the 6000 men arrested, 2400 were living in Montréal, and 3000 in Toronto. The rest were scattered across Canada. A month after war was declared, 5300 were released from jail on the condition that they report each month to the RCMP. The remaining 700 or so who were not released were eventually interned at the Petawawa army base 130 kilometres northwest of Ottawa. They included 236 men from Montréal.

The RCMP's two-day sweep in Montréal resulted in the arrest of 2400 Italian males, 236 of whom would be interned in Petawawa.

Individuals were rounded up by the RCMP or the police, pursuant to a federal Order-in-Council which called for "the registration of enemy aliens and the prohibition against the possession or use of firearms to all persons of German or Italian racial origins who have become naturalized British subjects since September 1, 1929."

Another 17000 Canadian people of Italian background, including women and children, were fingerprinted, photographed and ordered to report every month to the RCMP.

In the end, the *Defence Of Canada Regulations* resulted in the registration of 82500 "enemy aliens," 31000 of whom were of Italian origin.

The government created the position of The Custodian Of Alien Property, which empowered it to confiscate property and all business possessions of these so-called "enemy aliens," and to sell everything for virtually pennies. This action ruined many Italian businessmen, many of whom were never able to recover.

To this day, there has been no financial remuneration to these Canadians of Italian descent for their losses.

When any individual was finally released, he was required to sign the following undertaking, which was almost an admission of guilt, a guilt for crimes which he had never been prosecuted and which he had not committed: "I undertake and promise that I will carefully observe and obey the laws of Canada and such rules and regulations as may especially be prescribed for my conduct by competent authorities, and that I will do no act nor will I encourage the doing of any act which might be of injury to the Dominion of Canada, the United Kingdom or any of His Majesty's Dominions or any of the allied or the associated powers."

The "reasonable grounds" required for internment by the Order-in-Council of June 10, 1940 in fact included suspicious reports by paid informers of dubious credibility; membership in associations with Italian names; and involvement with organizations roughly equivalent to the heritage language classes of today. Internment was at the discretion of the arresting authorities during raids. No motivation was offered; no defence possible; no information released except after the internment was complete.

Sunday, November 4, 1990, Prime Minister Brian Mulroney apologized at a luncheon of the National Congress of Italian Canadians for the mistreatment inflicted on Canadians of Italian origin during World War II.

No individual, either interned or registered, was ever charged.